Queuing and Waiting

Studies in the Social Organization of Access and Delay

Barry Schwartz

University of Chicago Press
Chicago and London

For Janet

The University of Chicago Press, Chicago 60637
The University of Chicago Press, Ltd., London

Library of Congress Cataloging in Publication Data

Schwartz, Barry, 1938–
    Queuing and waiting.

    Bibliography: p.
    Includes index.
    1. Time allocation.   2. Queuing theory.   3. Social
interaction.   I. Title.
HM73.S358   301.5   75–11607
ISBN 0–226–74210–5

Contents

iii

Acknowledgments

The research brought together in this volume was carried out over a period of three years. I profited during this time from valuable comments which Morris Janowitz, William J. Wilson, Peter Blau, Philip Blumstein, and Florence Levinsohn made on several of my papers. Charles Bidwell was especially generous in this respect. I am also obliged to those of my students who read and were stimulated by these papers.

Material assistance was not lacking. Charles Bidwell, current editor of the *American Journal of Sociology*, kindly allowed me to survey the journal's manuscript records. Access to Chicago emergency department and national medical survey data was made possible by Odin Anderson, Director of the Center for Health Administration Studies of the University of Chicago. The center also helped support my research in these health-related areas. The bulk of my support was provided by the Ford Foundation.

I also thank Charles Bosk, John Faris, Lynn Pettler, and David Romes, from whom I received competent fieldwork and computational assistance.

Caroline Wolf deserves a special acknowledgment. Without her totally voluntary interest and cooperation, as well as her excellent fieldwork, the research presented in chapter 6 would not have been possible.

Introduction

Many traditional societies furnish no equivalent for the English word "time"; their members consequently have no conception of what it is to be "on time" or to "wait." In a modern society, however, where order is the outcome of integrated scheduling and where productive and monetary value is assigned to systematically divided units of time, it becomes not only possible but, from a practical standpoint, also quite necessary for punctuality and delay to be reflected upon and to become serious concerns of everyday life.

Although we know comparatively little about the social organization of time, we have learned that growth in a society's product uses far more time than we originally had thought.[1] The prophecies made two decades ago about expanding leisure were wrong because we miscalculated the indirect consequences of production. We assumed that the technical efficiency of automation would give us more free time; in fact, we work as much now as we did thirty years ago, for needs, as always, have risen along with the level of technology. There is also the neglected issue of how busy a rising level of consumption would keep us. In an age of consumerism we find ourselves spending more time than ever making decisions about what to buy; in this age of affluence, we use up more time in the process of buying; and, in an era of quality control, when planned obsolescence has become an intrinsic feature of rational economics, we discover that our goods require increasingly expensive and time-consuming maintenance. Hence the new realization that consumption is never over and done with in an instant.

Furthermore, as the product and wealth of a society increase, its population demands more services, most of which are obtained during the nonwork or so-called leisure hours. For these, too, time is expended. Decisions must be made concerning which server or service to use, while procurement of the service itself involves travel time and delay. Accordingly, as the service sector outstrips the productive sphere of the economy, we make more appointments and waste more time waiting for them to come about.

Thus, time has become scarce during our recent past because it is increasingly bound up with growing consumption of goods and services. The latter have in turn diminished what they were supposed to enrich: there is less real leisure because we now allocate so much of our time to consuming and to maintaining (or working to maintain) what we consume. In other words, modern means of production, distribution, and service have given us more to do in the face of a fixed amount of time to do it in. But new demands on an inelastic supply of time can only raise its value; hence the phobia of time waste and preoccupation with efficient scheduling—and this in an era when rising demand renders punctual forms of social organization most problematic. In the post-industrial age of mass consumption, waste of time has therefore become a dominant source of anxiety.

The expansion of goods and services has also affected the organization of economic life, which has in turn intensified aversion toward time waste. Because the satisfaction of massive demand requires foreseeable modes of supply, dispensers of goods and services must pursue their work during specific, predictable parts of the day. Standardization in this respect places very definite restrictions on the extent to which individuals can place themselves at one another's disposal; it then becomes increasingly necessary for service personnel and their clientele to arrange appointments on the basis of probable duration of service and mutual availability of time. This sort of arrangement can be a very precarious thing. The very fact that a person may fill all or part of his working day by providing service at, say, ten- to fifteen-minute intervals, makes it necessary for his clients to think in terms of time limits which are at least as narrow as his. For, to be as little as a half hour late might create expensive idle time for a server and could also delay other clients. Similarly, delays on the part of a server interfere with a client's subsequent appointments and so impinge on his already committed time. To minimize these contingencies, conceptions of time must be precise enough to correspond to the temporal work structure of service units. The imperative of punctuality and its constraints on delay are thus grounded, at the organizational level, in functional necessity, and are sustained in routine interaction among servers and clients.

It would seem redundant to claim that systems whose achievements are dependent upon the precise coordination of activities tend to organize these activities in a way that minimizes wasteful delay. Experience tells us, however, that punctuality is less than absolute and not equally binding on all parties. In fact, the modern order, with its enlarged service sector and precariously complex organization, furnishes unlimited opportunities for what often seems to be unlimited periods of waiting. We queue up for unscheduled service at the supermarket, the post office, and the theater; we wait at barber shops and restaurants, at stoplights, tollbooths, and, lately, gasoline stations. At the racetrack we line up to place bets and collect winnings. We also wait for supposedly scheduled trains, buses, and planes—after waiting to buy tickets and check our baggage. For those who repair our homes we wait, as we do for those who would repair us. And just as our calendars are thick with appointments with unpunctual people who will keep us waiting, so they contain the names of those whose fate is to be delayed by our own tardiness. As for the few who would rise up and protest their delay, they will find the lines to the complaint department busy and long.

It has been said that societies can only generate within themselves such problems as are within their capacity to solve. So it is with the modern order, in which we already find one framework for the analysis and control of delay and congestion. The systematic investigation of queuing actually began in 1913 when Erlang formulated a mathematical model of caller delays in Copenhagen's telephone circuits. Since then, mathematical queuing theory has become a basic tool of operations research and is presently applied to a variety of problems ranging from canal and airplane runway congestion, fluctuations in inventories and automobile traffic, to movement of customers through ticket counters, cafeterias, and medical facilities. (For more examples, see Saaty 1961.)

However sophisticated mathematical formulations of the queuing process may be, they rest upon a very simple assumption: given a "service model" (e.g., single queue-single server, single queue-multiple servers, etc.) and a priority rule or "queue discipline" (e.g., service in accordance with appointment, type of need, order of arrival, etc.), variations in queue size and waiting time are determined by (1) an organization's arrival distribution and (2) its service time distribution. Accordingly, estimates of waiting time may be derived by simulation methodology for any value or combination of values or specifications with regard to these parameters.

This kind of formal analysis makes possible a precise description of queuing phenomena; however, it does not allow for their understanding. For this we must design a series of investigations that will transcend descriptive input-output schemata and reveal the underlying *social* organization of access and delay. We need to inquire into the institutional constraints which maintain observable server-arrival (i.e., supply-demand) ratios. We should know what motivational and organizational factors enter into the determination of a server's work rate. How are orderly queues sociologically possible, and what institutional and cultural elements go into the formulation of priority rules? Another problem has to do with the meanings conferred upon time by servers and clients and how they mediate the relationship between delay and its costs. These are some of the basic questions the present group of studies will pose and try to answer. They do so with a view to establishing a sociology of queuing and waiting.

Overview

The above questions may be reduced to three specific points of reference, which organize the contents of this book. These relate to sources of variation in (1) waiting time; (2) the internal organization and order of queues; and (3) the manner in which delay is interpreted by clients and servers. Each of these general problems is addressed by two or more separate investigations.

Sources of Delay

The first chapter, "Waiting, Exchange, and Power: The Distribution of Time in Social Systems," attempts to formulate on a theoretical level the relationship between location in a social structure and the expenditure of waiting time. A dominant assumption of this article, and one which informs the volume as a whole, is that waiting limits productive uses of time and in so doing generates distinct social and personal costs. The specific purpose of the paper is to show how these costs are distributed throughout the social system and to identify the principles to which this allocation gives expression. The main proposition is that the distribution of waiting time coincides with the distribution of power. This proposition is based on the assumption that an individual's power reflects the scarcity of the goods or skills he possesses; accordingly, the relationship between a server and client may be characterized in terms of organized dependency, for which waiting (under certain conditions) provides an accurate index. Waiting time is thus conceived to be the product of a competitive process: clients bring their resources to bear to compete with one another for access to a service; organizations and individual servers accommodate clients in accordance with market pressure to compete for them. However, the paper goes on to show, if delay is related to the client's position in a power network, then he may show deference to a server by an expressed willingness to wait, or a server may confirm or enhance his own status by deliberately causing him to wait. Secondary interactional modes thus come to amplify a relationship originally grounded in a supply-demand structure. The broader implications of this correlation will allow us to characterize stratification systems in terms of the apportionment of time as well as the distribution of other kinds of resources.

The last half of "Waiting, Exchange, and Power" is an initial statement on a more general problem, namely, the extent to which delay is governed by the simple ratio of servers to clients. The two empirical papers in part 1 extend this line of inquiry. Using data from a sample of medical facilities in a large metropolitan area, "Emergency Department Structure and Waiting Time" (chapter 2) shows that under a given level of client demand, delay is more dependent upon the organization of service than on its actual magnitude. The paper also demonstrates complex interactions among these three factors in the determination of client waiting time. Chapter 3, "Manuscript Queues and Editorial Organization," documents the same principle in a longitudinal study of a single organization. It shows that increases in the size of a work queue have distinctly different effects on the waiting time of its elements in different stages of the editorial process. This study describes the way organizational constraints, expressed through a functionally necessary task hierarchy, condition the impact of increased input, and explains why we never find a direct correspondence between size of the manuscript queue and manuscript waiting time.

In brief, the three investigations in part 1 indicate very clearly that an analysis of the queuing process is incomplete without recognition of its structural and interactional as well as its simple supply-demand contingencies.

Priorities in Client Processing

The papers in the first section of this volume rest on the unstated assumption that queues are orderly. The general empirical merit of this assumption only raises the problem of how this order is possible. Chapter 4, "Queue Discipline," confronts that question directly. This essay explores the bases of the "normal rule" of first come, first served, the conditions which require exceptions to it, and the normative and situational contingencies which undermine its capacity to organize the demand for diverse services. Chapter 5, "Formal and Informal Priorities in an Emergency Medical Treatment System," goes beyond the matter of priority in general and deals with official and unofficial ways of ordering clients in an actual medical context. The paper seeks to identify the specific conditions under which considerations of social worth enter into client delay in a system which is officially committed to impersonal standards. The broader significance of these two papers is that they point to the many senses in which queuing, as a "control system," makes possible part of what we have come to know as public order. From a second, related, standpoint, they represent a line of departure for study of how different service organizations accommodate themselves through their "queuing policies" to varying levels and kinds of client demand.

The Meaning of Waiting

The title of this volume introduces a distinction between queuing and waiting. That difference relates to the purpose of part 3. The queue, whether it be lined or not, is a social structure consisting of elements organized in terms of priority; waiting, on the other hand, is an orientation of the personalities which constitute the "elements" of that structure. The study of delay is therefore a task requiring psychological as well as structural and interactional modes of analysis; it demands investigation of the subjective standpoints of clients and their servers. For, delay is not only suffered; it is also interpreted: it has meaning for both those who wait and those who keep them waiting.

The purpose of the first paper in this section, "Waiting, Deference and Distributive Justice" (chapter 6), begins with a simple assumption: that servers' valuation of a client's time varies in accordance with his social rank. Given the differential costs which clients incur through having to wait, a question is raised concerning the principles which govern the distribution of remedial deference an organization bestows in compensation for creating delays. The results show how the deference which servers exhibit toward these clients directly mirrors their interpretation of the value and meaning of clients' time.

Chapter 7, "Religious Variation in Client Impatience" addresses the problem of the meaning of waiting in two further ways. First, it concerns itself with the standpoint of the client; secondly, it deals with the cultural sources of his impatience. After showing that the concept of the "preciousness of time" has its origin in a now widely held religious ethic, this investigation draws on questionnaire responses to a nationwide survey on health care experience and attitudes to determine the extent to which this religious outlook continues to influence time orientations, as indexed by expressions of impatience during waits for medical service. The surprising results demonstrate how religious meanings may be superimposed upon the strictly economic or interactional significance of delay. The third chapter in this section, "Notes on the Social Psychology of Waiting," is a theoretical extension of the preceding empirical inquiries. Through an analysis of boredom and the degradational aspects of delay, this essay demonstrates further that more profitable activities foregone account for only part of the distress of waiting.

The papers we have just reviewed indicate that delay is related to important points of reference for the general analysis of social systems. The temporal coordination of activities, for example, is clearly an *integrative* problem. Because it makes possible the precise fitting together of diverse lines of action, we will find the clock to be an important regulatory mechanism in the integrative subsector of the social system. However, we shall see that the conditions of modern life introduce motivational as well as chronometrical imperatives; they demand not only a precise system of time accounting but also a universal and deeply installed respect for it. The latter finds its most direct expression in the norm of punctuality, whose internalization constitutes a problem in normative *pattern maintenance*. We will also find that a failure in the above sectors causes repercussions on the *adaptive* processes of the social system and upon its *goal attainment* functions as well (see Parsons and Smelser 1957). Such a paradigm is useful so far as it helps to articulate the fact that, in modern life, default of activity synchronization represents a "dysfunction" (at both the unit and system levels) whose cost is embodied in waiting time, which is the most direct and visible index of processual malintegration. However, a treatment of the neglected positive functions of waiting in the concluding essay, "Some Unappreciated Consequences of Delay" (chapter 9), causes us to qualify this standpoint in a number of important ways.

It should be apparent from the overview that the unity of this book resides not in consistency of conception, methodology, or context but in the dedication with which it pursues a single theme. A flexible approach like this is quite necessary. Because delay is so ubiquitous an aspect of social life, no single setting or point of view could possibly capture its multifaceted significance. To be most fully understood, the problem must be studied in a variety of locales and from different methodological and theoretical perspectives. Thus, the observational foci of this volume include medical settings, an editorial office, a mortgage company, and numerous other sites. The methodology ranges from survey analysis to ethnographic observation and the exploratory essay. Theoretical standpoints from which queuing and waiting are observed include formal organization and cultural and institutional analysis, on the one hand, and, on the other, exchange theory, psychoanalysis, collective behavior, and interactional social psychology. However, these diverse points of view are brought together and organized around a basic, two-sided, objective: the investigations represent a step toward the development of queuing and waiting as a special content area; and they inform the relationship between social structure and social process, which is a general issue of widespread and enduring concern.

1   Sources of Delay

1   Waiting, Exchange, and Power: The Distribution of Time in Social Systems

Delay and congestion are relevant to the analysis of social systems because they undermine the efficiency with which these systems conduct their business. Indeed, one Russian economist (Liberman 1968–69: 12–16) recently observed that because of its enormous cost in terms of more productive activities foregone, delay in waiting rooms and queues merits the status of a social problem. A gross estimate of the dimensions of this problem is furnished by Orlov, who reports that the Soviet population wasted about thirty billion hours a year waiting during their shopping tours alone. This is the equivalent of a year's work for no less than fifteen million people (*New York Times*, May 13, 1969: 17). Another study shows that monthly queuing for the payment of rent and utilities wastes at least twenty million man-hours a year in Moscow alone (*New York Times*, June 25, 1972: 23). If figures like these were aggregated for the entire service sector of the labor force, social inefficiency occasioned by clients' waiting would stand out even more dramatically.

Although the problem of delay may be more acute in some societies than in others, no modern society can claim immunity in this respect. Not only must every social system "decide" how much different members are to be given from a collective supply of goods and services, it must also decide the priority in which the members' needs are to be satisfied. Queuing for resources is in this sense a fundamental process of social organization, regardless of the specific level of its affluence. Indeed, though the amount of waiting time per unit consumption may be minimal in the richer, consumer-oriented societies, a higher volume of consumption leaves open the possibility that

Reprinted with permission from *American Journal of Sociology* 79 (January 1974): 841–71.

more time is lost in waiting under conditions of affluence than under conditions of scarcity.

On the other hand, it may be said that the social costs of waiting, no matter where they are incurred or what their absolute level may be, merely derive from the summation over an entire population of rather negligible individual losses. But this does not seem to be the case. As one American commentator (Bradford 1971: 82) puts it: "None of us would think of throwing away the nickels and quarters and dimes that accumulate in our pockets. But almost all of us do throw away the small-change time—five minutes here, a quarter hour there—that accumulates in any ordinary day. I figure I probably threw away a full working day in the dentist's office this past year, flicking sightlessly through old magazines." Even in the more opulent of modern societies, then, waiting time creates significant deficits for the individual as well as the system. At issue, however, is (1) the way such cost is distributed throughout a social structure and (2) the principles which govern this distribution. These questions are the subject of the present inquiry.

We begin with the assumption that delay is immediately caused by the relations of supply and demand: when the number of arrivals in some time unit is less than the maximum number an organization can accommodate, waiting time will be relatively brief; but if the arrival rate exceeds the service rate, a "bottleneck" is created and a longer waiting period results. Delay is in this sense occasioned by limitations of access to goods and services. However, this model does not explain socially patterned variations in waiting time. We must therefore explore the institutional constraints which sustain observable levels of scarcity and which organize the priorities granted to different groups of clients. These constraints are shown to be the expressions of existing power relations.

As we proceed, however, we discover that a purely structural model is tied to the very assumptions it seeks to extend, inasmuch as it takes objective scarcity as its point of departure. We then demonstrate how scarcities grounded in structured power relations may be deliberately magnified by the very people engaged in these relations. And so delay is found to be partially independent of supply and demand, in whose relation this variable was originally thought to find its exclusive source.

The above argument is informed by the assumption that time

is a general resource which may be expended productively or wastefully with respect to the acquisition of other, more particular advantages. As such, our analysis will not only help clarify the way "productive time" and "idle time" are allocated in a social system, it will also show how this distribution affirms and even reinforces that system's power arrangements.

Waiting, Scarcity, and Power

When economic exchange involves massive demand for specialized services, disturbances at the level of synchronization of supply and demand result in congestion. Waiting thus finds its organizational precondition in the scarcities occasioned by an advanced division of labor.

Waiting is related to scarcity in two respects. When the demand for a good or service exceeds its absolute supply, people may queue up before it is actually made available in order to ensure they will be accommodated. Others will wait with no guarantee of being served.[1] This latter condition is most widespread and conspicuous in the Soviet Union where, according to Orlov (New York Times, May 13, 1969: 17), an average shopper must often wait in long lines at three to five stores in order to buy the item he wants. The same kind of problem arises in more consumer-oriented countries during periods of peak demand, for example, intercity transportation during holidays, theaters and restaurants on weekends, bargain days in department stores, important sporting events, and so forth.

Regardless of the scarcity of a good, however, organizations tend to minimize the employment of servers; in doing so they minimize labor costs and enhance profits. Similarly, those who sell their skills tend to create queues so as to minimize their idle time. A second condition of waiting, then, is the ratio of supply of servers to demand for the services which they are prepared to offer. The fewer the servers in relation to the number of clients they must accommodate, the greater will be the average client's waiting time. Moreover, the greater the scarcity of a service, and the more inelastic the demand for that service, the less is a server compelled to reduce the waiting time of clients. Urgency of need thus minimizes the probability of "balking," that is, refusing to enter the queue, and "reneging," or abandoning the queue after having entered.

Waiting is patterned by the distribution of power in a social system. This assertion hinges on the assumption that power is directly associated with an individual's scarcity as a social resource and, thereby, with his value as a member of a social unit (see Blau 1964: 118). Accordingly, the person who desires a valued service generally cannot gain immediate access to its dispenser but must instead wait until others are accommodated.

However, it would probably be more precise to say that the capacity to make others wait is a property of roles and not their incumbents. The petty bureaucrat or cashier, for example, may himself possess little that is of value to others; however, he governs access to resources which are. As a result, he is able to keep people of great substance waiting for as long as he sees fit. Of course, when a server's power derives solely from his access to his employer's resources, that power can only be exercised over clients. In the absence of valued personal qualities his position in the organization itself will be a lowly one.

Waiting and Exchange

After a certain point, waiting becomes a source of irritation not only because it may in itself be wearisome, boring, and annoying, but also because it increases the investment a person must make in order to obtain a service, thereby increasing its cost and decreasing the profit to be derived from it. This loss to the waiter is related to the fact that time is a finite resource; its use in any particular way implies the renunciation of other rewards and opportunities. Put differently, in waiting, usable time becomes a resource that is typically nonusable. This transformation is mediated by the power relation between server and client: time, whose use is ordinarily governed only by the client—that is to say, expended for the sake of a benefit that he alone desires—is transformed during the waiting period into a resource that is governed only by the one whom the client attends.

However, the formal interactional properties of waiting are independent of vicissitudes in its personal cost. To be able to make a person wait is, above all, to possess the capacity to modify his conduct in a manner congruent with one's own interests. To be delayed is in this light to be dependent upon the disposition of the one whom one is waiting for. The latter, in turn, and by virtue of this dependency, finds himself further confirmed in his position of power. Looked at in a different way, it may be said that while having to wait may under certain conditions be negative and harmful to the interests of particular individuals, it often furthers the interests of those who keep them waiting. Waiting is therefore a negative condition only when we confine ourselves to the standpoint of the person who is delayed.

The one-sidedness of this statement may be balanced by two considerations which specify its applicability. First, the disadvantage of the waiter may be a detriment to the server as well. For, the benefits of waiting (such as respite from previous interaction and an opportunity to prepare for subsequent involvement) presumably shrink as the costs of activities foregone increase; their intersection constitutes grounds for the waiter to renege from the waiting channel without being served. Correspondingly, the benefits a server receives by keeping a particular client waiting may initially be of greater value to him than time spent serving that client; however, the declining value to the server of keeping that client waiting further and the rising cost entailed in delaying service also reach a point of intersection. This convergence constitutes grounds for offering service. The relationship between the first intersection and the second is crucial: if he is to stay busy, the server had better decide to serve before the client decides to leave. Although waiting represents an unfavorable exchange position for a client, the very principles which make it so subject the server to pressures which mitigate the extent of his delay. However, these pressures vary in terms of the scarcity and value of service, which suppress the probability of reneging. This leads back to our initial point that his scarcity enhances the exchange position of a valued server who, while needing clients, needs no particular client; he can therefore take his time about serving any one of them.

The Stationary Server

The highly advantageous position of the server is intensified when viewed in terms of a stationary server/mobile client model. This arrangement not only affirms the power of the former (for the latter must expend resources to come to obtain the service he offers) but also works to his advantage in other ways. First, the stationary server often has at hand sufficient opportunities for alternative involvement to offset the loss to which the tardiness of a client would otherwise subject him; second, he may have the power to schedule and thereby control the sequence and pace of his activity.

The latter advantage is most conspicuously instanced by the widespread practice (particularly common among physicians with a large following) of overscheduling—setting up two or more appointments at very narrow intervals in order to ensure that possible delays on the part of clients, or a run of quick services, will not leave the server with idle time. Yet, even when confronted with an empty waiting room the server has at his disposal enough alternative involvement materials to minimize his loss. These may involve "secondary queues," for example, paper work, checking of supplies, necessary calls to colleagues and clients, and so forth. On the other hand, the waiter is usually unable to transport enough supplies to keep himself maximally occupied, at least from a productive standpoint. Even the client who can bring his business to the waiting room in a briefcase may find himself unable to work comfortably in this strange and perhaps distracting setting. He is then cut off from queues which await *his* service.

Thus, by making the client wait, the server may often impose a loss without suffering one himself. On the other hand, by reneging, the client fails to impose a substantial loss upon a server, who may continue to operate productively; yet the client subjects himself to loss in terms of time already invested in waiting. Moreover, even when he is forced into idleness, the server may charge his clients for the time lost. This is especially true among psychiatrists, whose rigid 30- or 50-minute treatment sessions prevent them from overscheduling. On the other hand, when the popular server is delayed and forces his client into excessive idleness he does not consider it necessary to make compensation.[2]

Just as the mobile client may find himself at the mercy of a stationary server, the mobile server can be used hard by a stationary client. This server may have to wait until the client is ready to be seen and may get caught up in other people's queues—for instance, traffic jams that occur between visits to clients. Hence the increasing reluctance on the part of professionals to leave their offices for fieldwork and house calls. This practice redounds to their moral as well as material benefit, on the basis of the "if you want an audience, you come to *me*" principle (see Spencer 1886: 105). This seems to be confirmed by the fact that professionals generally do go to clients whose status exceeds their own. The doctor or lawyer who refuses to conduct business in the homes of the ordinary will more often than not rush to an ailing or wailing top executive, taking care not to keep him waiting.

On the other hand, there are some servers who by the very nature of their work are forced to be mobile. These include insurance agents, door-to-door salesmen, delivery men, messengers, repair men, subcontractors, and the like. Of these, it is perhaps the subcontractors who embody the clearest exception to the tendency for server mobility to be a disadvantage (Glaser 1972: 90–107). Because the popular building subcontractor can take on more work than he can finish directly, and then hold the customer by beginning a job he will finish at his own convenience, this type of server can make a virtue out of the absolute necessity of his mobility (but of course only while the market is in his favor).

Stratification of Waiting

Typical relationships obtain between the individual's position within a social system and the extent to which he waits for and is waited for by other members of the system. In general, the more powerful and important a person is, the more others' access to him must be regulated. Thus, the least powerful may almost always be approached at will; the most powerful are seen only "by appointment." Moreover, because of heavy demands on their time, important people are most likely to violate the terms of appointments and keep their clients waiting. It is also true that the powerful tend not to ask for appointments with their own subordinates; rather, the lowly are summoned—which is grounds for them to cancel their own arrangements so as not to "keep the boss waiting."

The lowly must not only wait for their appointments with superiors; they may also be called upon to wait during the appointment itself. This may be confirmed in innumerable ways. For one, consider everyday life in bureaucracies. When, in their offices, superordinates find themselves in the company of a subordinate, they may interrupt the business at hand to, say, take a phone call, causing the inferior to wait until the conversation is finished. Such interruption may be extremely discomforting for the latter, who may wish not to be privy to the content of the conversation but, having no materials with which to express alternative involvement, must wait in this exposed state until his superior is ready to reengage him. The event becomes doubly disturbing when the superior fails to recover from the distraction, loses his train of thought, and is unable to properly devote himself to the moment's business. Of course, the subordinate is demeaned not only by the objective features of this scene but also by his realization that for more important clients the superior would have placed an embargo on all incoming calls or visitors. He would have made others wait. The assumption that the client correctly makes is that his own worth is not sufficient to permit the superior to renounce other engagements; being unworthy of full engagement, he is seen, so to speak, between the superior's other appointments. In this way, the client is compelled to bear witness to the mortification of his own worthiness for proper social interaction.

While the derogatory implications for self are clear when the person must repeatedly step aside and wait until the superordinate decides that the granting of his time will not be excessively costly, debasement of self may be attenuated by the client's own consideration that his superior is, after all, in a position of responsibility and assailed by demands over which he may not exercise as much control as he would like. But even this comforting account may be unavailable when the server himself initiates the interruption. It is possible for him to make a call, for example, or to continue his work after the client enters, perhaps with the announcement that he will "be through in a minute."

It is especially mortifying when the superior initiates a wait when an engagement is in progress. Thus, a subordinate, while strolling along a corridor in conversation with his superior, may find himself utterly alone when the latter encounters a colleague and breaks off the ongoing relationship in his favor. The subordinate (who may not do the same when encountering one of his peers) is compelled to defer by standing aside and waiting until the unanticipated conversation is finished. Nothing less is expected by his superior, who, finding himself gaining less from the engagement than his inferior, assumes the right to delay or interrupt it at will if more profitable opportunities should arise.

The immunity of the privileged. The relationship between rank and accessibility implies that waiting is a process which mediates interchanges between those who stand on different sides of a social boundary. These divisions and the rules of access which correspond to them are found in organizations which are themselves bounded with respect to the outside world. This fact raises the problem of access when outsiders or clients (as well as insiders, that is, employees or coworkers) seek contact with persons situated at different points in a service hierarchy:

> Low down on the scale are the men you can walk right up to. They are usually behind a counter waiting to serve you on the main floor, or at least on the lower floors. As you go up the bureaucracy you find people on the higher floors and in offices: first bullpens, then private offices, then private offices with secretaries — increasing with each step the inaccessibility and therefore the necessity for appointments and the opportunity to keep people waiting. Recently, for example, I had an experience with a credit card company. First, I went to the first floor where I gave my complaint to the girl at the desk. She couldn't help me and sent me to the eighth floor to talk to someone in a bullpen. He came out, after a suitable waiting time, to discuss my problem in the reception room. I thought that if I were to straighten this matter out I was going to have to find a vice-president in charge of something, who would keep me waiting the rest of the day. I didn't have time to wait so I took my chances with said clerk, who, of course, didn't come through. I'm still waiting for the time when I have an afternoon to waste to go back and find that vice-president to get my account straightened out.[3]

The above statement suggests that delaying a typical client may be a prerogative of important servers. However, we must also recognize that powerful clients are relatively immune from waiting. This remark accords with Tawney's (1931: 229) emphasis on the asymmetry of power relations. "Power," he writes, "may be defined as the capacity of an individual, or group of individuals, to modify the conduct of other individuals or groups in the manner which he desires, *and to prevent his own conduct being modified in the manner in which he does not*" (emphasis added).

The relative immunity from waiting which the powerful enjoy is guaranteed because they have the resources to refuse to wait; that is, because they can often afford to go elsewhere for faster service or cause others, such as servants or employees, to wait in their places. Thus, while the relationship between privilege and the necessity of waiting cannot be generalized in any deterministic way, there nevertheless appears to be a relationship between the two, with the least-privileged clients compelled to do the most waiting. This general statement is consistent with Mann's (1969: 353) more specific observations regarding the stratification of waiting in lined queues:

> The relationship between cultural equality and public orderliness is attenuated in the area of queuing because waiting in line is not a habit of all social classes in Western society. It is reasonable to suppose that if Mrs. Gottrocks joined a theater or a football line in the United States, Australia, or England, she would not be treated differently than anyone else, but it would be a rare event for someone of Mrs. Gottrocks's status to use a line. Ordinarily, in both class-conscious and relatively class-free societies, the privileged class circumvent the line altogether and get their tickets through agents or other contacts.[4] Our point, then is that queuing is confined largely to the less-privileged groups in society.

The privileged also wait less because they are least likely to tolerate its costs; they are more inclined to renege from, as well as balk at, entering congested waiting channels. On the other hand, the less advantaged may wait longer not only because of their lack of resources but also because their willingness to wait exceeds the readiness of those in higher strata. While they might have something else to do besides sitting and waiting, they might not have anything better to do. As a result, the least advantaged may pay less in profitable alternatives foregone and therefore suffer less loss than even those whose objective wait is shorter.

This relationship may be informed by another consideration, for which health-care delivery systems provide an example. Because of the scarcity of health services, those who are able to pay for medical services are often forced to wait well beyond the time a server agreed to provide them. Yet there is some limit to the server's inconsiderateness, for, in principle at least, the client may decide that he has waited long enough and go elsewhere. On the other hand, those who are unable to pay for medical care may spend the better part of the day in outpatient waiting rooms, for consideration of the value of clients' time is far less imperative when these clients cannot take their business to someone else. In Britain's government-run maternity hospitals, for example, "a major complaint was that women dependent on the health service are treated offhandedly in hospitals and frequently have to wait more than an hour for checkups at antenatal clinics. Women who paid up to $700 for private treatment were dealt with speedily and efficiently" (*Chicago Tribune*, June 12, 1971: 10). Thus, while long, agonizing waiting periods may be avoided only if one is willing to settle for more expensive service, the poor may avoid waiting only if they are willing to settle for no service at all. (The frequency with which they do select this option is, of course, unknown—as is the consequence of the selection.)

The above principle may be further illustrated in other, altogether different, connections. It is noticeable, for example, that in the "best" of urban department stores a customer is met by a salesperson as soon as he enters; the customer makes a selection under his guidance and makes payment to him. In establishments which are a grade below the best, customers may have difficulty finding someone to serve them during busy periods but, when they do, are accompanied by him, that is, "waited on," until the transaction is consummated by payment. The lowest-grade stores, however, provide few servers; as a result, customers must for the most part wait on themselves, then line up behind others at a cashier counter in order to make payment.

The above patterns are to be observed within as well as among organizations. In the typical department store, customers surveying high-priced goods like furniture and appliances will typically be approached immediately by a salesperson. Those in the process of selecting a handkerchief or pair of socks will not be so quickly attended and, when they finally are, will be dealt with more quickly. Likewise, clients who show interest in very expensive jewelry will be served at once and at length; those who are fascinated with costume jewelry will wait.

In general, it may be said that establishments which cater to a relatively wealthy clientele must serve them quickly (if the clients desire) not only because of the objective or assumed value of clients' time but also because they have the means to take their business elsewhere if it is not respected. Commercial places which serve the less wealthy are less constrained in this respect because they tend to deal with a larger and/or less independent clientele. Within organizations, clients who promise to bring the most profit to a server enjoy a competitive advantage; they wait the least, to the disadvantage of their lesser endowed brethren who can find no one to honor the value of their time.[5]

Waiting and the Monopolization of Services

The above rule, however, rests on the assumption that faster alternative services are available to those who want and can pay for them. In fact, the availability of such alternatives is itself variable. Waiting is therefore affected not only by clients' resources and consequent ability to go elsewhere for service but also by the opportunity to do so.

It follows that establishments with many competitors are most likely to be concerned about the amount of time they keep clients waiting. Chicago Loop banks are among such organizations. In the words of one banking consultant, "The industry is too competitive to allow a dozen people waiting in line when they could just as easily take their business across the street where there is a teller at every window, a customer at every teller and waiting time is less than one minute" (*Chicago Tribune*, September 28, 1971: 7). However, organizations with few or no competitors are less obliged to reduce the waiting time of clients. (This condition makes waiting a national pastime in the Soviet Union, where most services are rendered by government-run establishments that are not subject to market forces.)

The enormous amounts of waiting time expended in dealings with public people-serving bureaucracies is directly related to

monopolization of the various services which they offer or impose. Monopolization accords governmental units the power to maximize their efficiency of operation by minimizing service costs and, in so doing, maximizing client waiting. This "optimum solution" is exemplified by bureaus which distribute welfare benefits to long lines of disadvantaged people:

> The number of Medicaid and public assistance applicants and recipients has become so great that [New York's] Department of Social Services is literally shutting its doors in their faces.
> Many of the 45 social service centers close their doors early — 12 or 1 or 2 o'clock — rather than admit persons the workers realistically know cannot be seen that particular day.
> The Medicaid office advises applicants to line up outside the doors before dawn. "You'd better get down here around 6:30 or 7 o'clock," said the person answering the telephone at the Medicaid office.... "We can only see 200 persons a day. If you want to be in the first 200 you better get here then — with your application filled out." The Medicaid office does not open until 8:30 a.m....
> Last week the department announced it had saved $39 million by employing fewer case workers. (*New York Times*, November 21, 1971: 58)

However, the relatively wealthy as well as the poor are put to inconvenience by having to wait in person for licenses, permits, visas, tickets, information, and the like. Dealings with government-sponsored transportation facilities can also be cited as an example:

> Before Amtrak took over, I would have to call the Illinois Central to go to Miami. If I wanted to go to New York, I'd call the Penn Central. To go west, the Santa Fe. But, now, under the streamlined, tax-supported Amtrak, one number, one central office, makes the reservations. They have computers and other modern devices the old system didn't have.
> At 10 minutes after noon, I dialed the new Amtrak reservation number. The line was busy, so I hung up and waited a few minutes and dialed again. It was still busy. Five minutes later, I tried again. It was busy. By 1 o'clock I had tried 10 times, and had heard only busy signals.
> Enough was enough. I phoned the Amtrak executive office,

to ask what was wrong with their reservation number. A woman there put me on hold. I was on hold for seven minutes. Then when she finally took me off hold, she switched me to somebody's office, and a secretary laughed and said: "Oh, yes, our lines are very busy."

At 2 p.m. it finally happened. Instead of getting a busy signal, it rang. It actually rang. . . . It rang. And it rang. And it rang. For eight minutes it rang. . . . So I hung up, got another cup of coffee and tried again. That was a mistake, because I heard another busy signal.

Then at 2:47 it happened. It rang. And somebody answered. I listened closely to make sure it wasn't a recorded message. No, it was really somebody alive. After that it was easy. In about eight or nine minutes the reservations were made.

The clock said 3 p.m. So I have to congratulate Amtrak. It took me only two hours and 50 minutes to complete a telephone call and make reservations. It would have probably taken me at least 10 minutes more than that to take a cab to O'Hare, board a plane, fly to Miami, and get off the plane. (*Chicago Daily News*, June 9, 1972: 3)

This instance is an especially informative one, for it demonstrates that the amount of time clients of an organization are called upon to wait is in large measure determined by the broader competitive structure in which that organization is situated. Longitudinal and cross-sectional means are brought to bear in this assessment. By reference to the temporal barrier to access to rail service after centralization and monopolization, relative ease of access before the transformation is implicitly affirmed. And after documenting the lengthy waiting time required in a noncompetitive service market, we find explicit reference to the ready availability of service offered in highly competitive ones (airlines, in this case). In this double sense, the institutional grounding of waiting time is a conclusion warranted by the facts.

We now turn to public services which by their very nature admit of no alternatives and which at the same time are so organized as to constitute the most radical instance of the principle we are now discussing.

A day in court. Discrepancy between demand for and supply of "authoritative judgment" is perhaps the most notorious source of waiting for both rich and poor. In fact, those who look forward to their "day in court," whether civil, criminal, or juvenile, very often find themselves spending their day in the courthouse corridor (many courts do not provide waiting rooms). In some courts, in fact, all parties whose cases are scheduled to be heard on a particular day are instructed to be present at its beginning when the judge arrives.[6] This is a most pronounced manifestation of what we earlier referred to as "overscheduling," which in this case ensures that the judge (whose bench is separated from his office or working area) will not be left with idle time that cannot be put to productive use—a consideration which may help us understand the seemingly irrational practice of assembling together at the beginning of the day those who are to be served during its course. While this tactic guarantees that the judge's valuable time will not be wasted, it also ensures that most parties will be kept waiting for a substantial period of time; some, all day long. Indeed, because they have no means to retaliate against the judge's own tardiness or excessive lunch breaks, some individuals may not be served at all and must return on the next day to wait further. Clients' attorneys, incidentally, keep them company during much of this time—a service for which the former pay dearly.

All of this is not to say that the organization of justice profits. It must, on the contrary, pay a very high price for support of its prima donnas. As one juvenile-court officer puts it:

> Waiting to be called into court . . . is the most serious problem. Just from an internal point of view this means that a probation counselor usually accomplishes nothing in the hour or more he often has to wait to get his case into court. Usually during this waiting period he sees no people, does no counselling, can't do dictation or other "desk-work"—his wait is complete, unproductive waste. These same problems apply to other professional people: caseworkers from the Department of Social Services, school principals, lawyers, etc.   (Fairfax County [Virginia] Juvenile and Domestic Relations Court, Memorandum, 1971: 1)

While attorneys[7] and other professionals are fortunate enough to claim a fee for doing nothing in a professional way, others are often denied this luxury. Authorities who are mindful of civil security, for example, wisely find it more expedient to dismiss cases (particularly such misdemeanants as traffic violators) for lack of witnesses and evidence than to tie up a large sector of the police force for the better part of the day in a crowded corridor. In this particular sense, the police are too important—their time too valuable—to be kept waiting. On the other hand, it may be claimed that by tying up defendants all day long in these same corridors justice may be served—provided, of course, that the defendants are in fact guilty as charged. However, the situation is quite different in felony cases, where casual dismissals are less probable. Under these circumstances police wait as long as defendants. In the Chicago gun court, for example, "40 or 45 police are waiting to testify at 9:30 a.m., when court begins. Cases are not scheduled for specific times, so most of them wait and wait. One recent day 31 were still waiting around at 1 p.m. The next day 20 were there at 1 p.m. And 23 the following day." The same conditions prevail at the narcotics court, where police waiting time "translates on an annual basis to 13,000 police days lost and $700,000 in expenses" (*Chicago Daily News*, August 21, 1973: 14).

Two observations emerge from and transcend the particular content of what has just been said. First, the assertion that clients may pay a high price, in terms of time, in their dealings with public bureaucracies means that a societal cost, expressed in terms of aggregate client time diverted from more productive activities, must be written into the usually implicit but sometimes explicit "optimum solution formulae" by which particular "public service" organizations maximize their own efficiency. Because of this factor, the real cost of governmental services is not to be understood in terms of budgetary considerations alone.

Second, minimization of a powerful server's idle time may subtract from the productivity of the organization as well as its clients. This observation, which is merely grotesquely evident in court settings, reflects the general principle that increments in efficiency in one part of a social organization often entail malfunction in other sectors. Accordingly, just as high concentration of power in an organization may lend itself to societal inefficiency, indexed by more productive client-time foregone, so concentration of power and honor in an elevated server may render organizations ineffective by maximizing idle time of subordinated servers. The more general import of this statement is that it amends the overly simplistic scarcity theory of waiting, which fixates our attention upon server shortage as a condition of client delay. The present statement shows that the organization of services, as well as their volume, provides occasion for waiting.

An additional point is that some persons and groups are relatively exempt from waiting. If we turn our attention once more to the courtroom, we find that the powerful are most likely to enjoy such advantage. In making up the docket, for example, resources are taken into account. Defendants who are represented by an attorney are very often scheduled before those who are not (in Chicago traffic courts, at least). And cases involving important and powerful contestants, witnesses, and/or lawyers may be scheduled at their convenience and not be delayed for long periods of time. Similarly, attorneys who enjoy favor with the court clerk are also able to avoid long waits because they are allowed to schedule their cases early.[8] Thus, while waiting time may be maximized by persons or organizations which enjoy full or near monopoly on the services they offer, the relationship between the power and waiting time of clients is probably attenuated rather than negated. For, while the powerful may lack the opportunity to take their business elsewhere, they nevertheless possess the resources to ensure that their needs will be accommodated before the needs of those with fewer means.

The resource-availability theory. In summary, the relationship between servers' and clients' power in relation to waiting is asymmetrical. On the one hand, servers' holding power is contingent on clients' inability to frequent more distant and/or expensive servers; on the other, client autonomy requires the presence of alternative services. Despite their covariation, though, resources and alternatives seem to affect waiting time independently of one another. The resourceful wait less within both monopolistic and competitive organizations; regardless of clients' resources, however, waiting time tends to be longer in monopolistic settings. This "resource-availability theory" of waiting may also help explain the varying "optimum solutions" adopted by diverse organizations seeking the most profitable balance between losses due to keeping clients waiting and the expense of additional servers. While the theory predictably suggests that the balance arrived at reflects the relative power of organizations or individual servers, it also holds such resolutions to be "zero sum" in nature. This is most evident in monopolistic, "public service" bureaucracies or among charismatic officials who maximize the efficiency of their operation at great organizational and social cost, expressed in terms of productive time lost through waiting. The optimization of unit interests is thus often brought about at the expense of system interests.

However, the resource-availability theory must be qualified by recognizing existing limitations on monopolies' capacity to restrict service. For despite their freedom from competition, monopolies must get their work done, lest their managing personnel be subjected to pressures from those who have the power to exert them. While monopolistic enterprises may not be responsive to their clients' evaluations, they are often subject to officials, such as elected representatives, who are not free to ignore these clients. If this is so, then the greater the number of people who are dependent upon a monopolized service, the more effective will be the pressure for its public regulation. Thus, while the telephone company is a monopoly, it does not enjoy unlimited freedom to reduce service and delay callers. The same can be said of the postal service (which is in fact sometimes overstaffed because it is a nest for political patronage) and other public utilities. Waiting time, then, is affected by political as well as economic constraints.

Social Psychological Aspects of Delay

On the psychological level, what has been said may be recapitulated in the following terms. The person who is delayed is not merely in a condition of objective dependence and subordination; because his only duty is to attend the call of a server, the waiter feels dependent and subordinate. To be kept waiting—especially to be kept waiting for an unusually long while—is to be the subject of an assertion that one's own time (and, therefore, one's social worth) is less valuable than the time and worth of the one who imposes the wait. This is why objections to being kept waiting sometimes take the form, "Why should I wait for him? My time is as valuable as his!" The actually inferior feeling that often gives rise to such a protest is especially common in such places as crowded waiting rooms, wherein each client, confronting multiple reflections of himself, is more pointedly made aware of his suppliant status and of how utterly insignificant he is as compared with the person for whom he waits. Of course, waiting does not create the sense of subordination but only accentuates an initial inferiority, which is often presupposed by the fact that one is waiting in the first place. It needs to be said that this same sentiment has its parallel on the other side of the relationship, for the server calls out in himself the responses that he elicits in the ones he keeps waiting, which enables him not only to be conscious of his own power—to see himself from the point of view of his clients—but also to feel within himself the independent power that he extracts from those who wait for him.

Waiting as a Determinant of the Value of Service

The above statement is one elaboration on a theme to which we have tried to adhere throughout this report, namely, that waiting presupposes and occurs within an established context of power relations and is to be understood in terms of these relations. Power, to repeat, entails among other things the capacity to provide scarce services which people must wait to receive. The significance of the service for the individual and the social power of the dispenser therefore hinges on its desirability.

"The only relevant question apart from the direct enjoyment of things for their qualities," wrote Simmel (1971: 68), "is the question of the way to them. As soon as this way is a long and difficult one, involving sacrifice in patience, disappointment, toil, inconvenience, feats of self-denial, etc., we call the object scarce. One can express this directly: things are not difficult to obtain because they are scarce, but they are scarce because they are difficult to obtain." Accordingly, if we regard waiting for a scarce service as an investment or sacrifice in return for a gain, we may measure part of the value of the gain by assessing the degree of sacrifice occasioned on its behalf. In Simmel's (1970: 23) words, "Valuation arises from the fact that something must be paid for things: the patience of waiting . . . the renunciation of things otherwise desirable."

The subjective value of the gain is therefore given not only by the objective value of the service but also by the amount of time invested in its attainment. This being the case, one may wait for another not only because he is a source of value; the other's service becomes valuable (and he becomes powerful) precisely because he is waited for. While analytically distinct, the two parts of this phenomenon are empirically inseparable. What is more important is that they are functionally inseparable; this is to say that waiting subserves the distribution of power that it presupposes. It does so in two interrelated senses: a common willingness to wait for a service sustains its objective scarcity which, in turn, transforms itself (as we have seen) into a subjective value. This principle is particularly clear in its negative aspect: in the observation that services to which we have immediate access—which we can acquire without waiting—are of relatively little value to us. It is known, for example, that in seeking professional help from a person with whom he is unacquainted, the client does not always rejoice at being granted an immediate appointment, nor at finding an empty waiting room when he arrives for this appointment. Such ease of access may speak unfavorably of the server's scarcity as a social or economic resource; it may disconfirm the worth of his service. In contrast, those who confront obstacles to service tend to have more confidence in its value, once it is acquired.

The above principle holds within but not outside of specific time limits. Beyond their upper boundary, a desired and valued service may be considered unattainable, and an otherwise willing client might just give up and renege. Those who choose to wait it out beyond that limit may, in so doing, find their estimation of the service to be actually lowered. This is because persons tend not only to place a higher value on services for which they must wait; they also demand more in proportion as they wait. After a certain point, the latter tendency may outweigh the former, raising expectations to such a level as to render their satisfaction impossible. The reward then cannot possibly be worth waiting for, let alone enhanced by waiting for it.

It follows that if services acquirable without waiting are of little value to us, those who wait to service us may be attributed a negative value; these servers become our subordinates.

Simmel put this more generally by saying: "We perceive the specific value of something obtained without difficulty as a gift of fortune only on the grounds of the significance which things have for us that are hard to come by and measured by sacrifice. It is the same value, but with the negative sign" (1971: 54). The original meaning of the term "waiter" accords with this formula. The waiter is, in this earlier sense, one who stands by, alert to the call and ready to respond to the demand of a superordinate. What the waiter waits for, then, is a command; he is, as the French expression makes clear, an *attendant*: one who caters to the whims of the ascendant. This earlier, courtly reference to waiting as a form of subordination is found even today (as a "survival," so to speak) in southeastern parts of the United States where we observe the very common substitution of "waiting *on*" (someone or other) in place of "waiting *for*." The mere transformation of the linguistic meaning of waiting, from a readiness to serve to a readiness to be served, has therefore not fully negated its essential sociological property: to wait on others and to be kept waiting exhibit the common element of subordination.

We have digressed in order to demonstrate the inverse case of a principle to which we now return; namely, that waiting is not simply a barrier to service but is rather the very condition of its subjective value. This idea must be addressed in further detail because it appears to contradict our earlier assertion that waiting is inimical to profit in social exchange. It now seems that the reduction of waiting time would not necessarily increase profit for a client (in an exchange with a server) because the value of that which is attended is itself dependent, at least in part, upon the very length of attendance. But from this an absurd hypothesis is deduced: that persons faced with the alternative of, say, a long and a short queue will join the longer one in order to enhance the value of what they will receive at the end of it (much as an individual might extend his foot from under a blanket on a cold night in order to enjoy the warmth that its withdrawal will provide). Absurd as it appears, there is some truth in this; but only in the following, limited sense: that those who wait the longest tend to value what they receive the most. But this only means that the subjective value of the service, that is, its value for the waiter, is positively modified in the very act of waiting, even though waiting itself is not desired, or, more precisely, simply because it is not desired. Therefore, the contradiction between this principle and the earlier one, which finds waiting to subtract from the profitability of an exchange with a server, is resolved by the term subjective value, to which the objective observer would be quite indifferent.

Making Others Wait

That waiting (within the limits referred to) will render a service more valuable, independently of its objective worth, seems to be an inherent feature of the psychology of social exchange. This property is perhaps made most intelligible by the principle of cognitive balance, which, according to Alexander and Simpson (1964: 182–92), tends to equilibrate psychological investment and profit (for a more general statement, see Festinger 1957). However, Simmel's was the first systematic discussion of this principle. His treatment is summarized in the observation that "even if objects or services possess no intrinsic ... interest, a substitute for this is furnished by the mere difficulty of acquiring them: they are worth as much as they cost. It then comes to appear that they cost what they are worth."

We may turn to an important implication of this principle. Because the worth of a person is not independent of the amount of time others must wait for him, that person can maintain and dramatize his worth by purposely causing another to wait.

Of course, the imposition of a waiting period does not in itself make a person or his services valuable; it can only magnify existing positive evaluations or transform neutral feelings into positive ones. If these initial feelings are not favorable, or at least neutral, the waiting caused by a server may lower clients' estimations of his worth. Instead of a sought-after and important man, the server becomes an incompetent who cannot perform his job properly; thus is his initial inferiority confirmed. (This is why subordinates who know where they stand do not like to keep their superiors waiting.) Generally, the dramatization of ascendency by keeping another waiting will do a server the most good when his social rank exceeds that of his client or when the difference between their ranks is ambiguous. In the latter case, ascendency accrues to him who can best dramatize it; in the former, ascendency may be dramatized by him to whom it already accrues.

Thus, just as authority is affirmed by the placement of social distance between super and subordinate, so temporal distance subserves the ascendency of the person who imposes it. More precisely, the restriction of access to oneself by forcing another to "cool his heels" is instrumental to the cultivation of social distance. The importance of this point resides in its inconsistency with the assumption that waiting is primarily dependent upon the supply of servers and demand for their services. The kind of waiting to which we now call attention is "ritual waiting," imposed without reference to scarcity of server time.

Now, ritual waiting is a form of mystification.

Waiting and Mystification

Causing another to wait is a form of "mystification" (see Goffman 1959: 67–70) because self-imposed restriction on accessibility underscores a server's scarcity and social value, thereby promoting awe among those who wait for him. Notwithstanding our own attempt at elaboration and extension, however, this line of thought does not take us far enough. For, if the reverence in which a server is held is to be profoundly felt, it must rest not only upon the server's essentially negative capacity to regulate access to himself but also upon his more positive ability to satisfy needs or alleviate tension within the person waiting for him. In holding himself apart, then, the charismatic server must also "do something" for the client. Furthermore, if whatever is done is to dazzle the client, its efficacy must apparently derive from the very person of the server, independently of the particular substantive benefits he is capable of providing. The latter, it might seem to the client, flow from the status of the server, but not from his specific individuality.

This consideration enables us to see in the ability to make others wait an ideal resource for mystification. For, when, after he has waited some time, a client's turn is finally called, the summons itself fulfills a need which, having been generated by the distress of waiting for a service, can have nothing to do with the need for the service itself. It may be argued that the distinction between these two sources of tension is merely of analytic worth; that, empirically, they merge insofar as the waiting period may exacerbate anxiety over the condition that requires service. But this objection only confirms the fact that by simply making himself available, the server can display a remarkable personal capacity to alleviate suffering. Because he is so intensely waited for, his very appearance makes us feel better. Hence the impression of an inherent power to relieve stress. (In this regard, see Bettelheim 1960: 87.) Because he is explicitly defined as the one to wait for (with all the messianic implications of such definition), the tension attending the wait can be relieved in no way other than through his appearance.

Lest it appear that the delay creates rather than enhances attraction, we should stress that the above statements are preconditioned by a server's initial appeal. In this connection, an additional qualification must be made. Causing a delay will not only fail to enhance the status of an unattractive server; it will also fail to elevate the server who cannot conceal from a client the fact that he is deliberately making him wait. For, if the object of imposing a delay is to give the impression of important business when none really exists, then the initial sense of awe must turn into infuriation when the mystery of power is seen through.

Servers who do not serve. In suggesting that a server may dramatize the scarcity and value of his skills by making others wait for him, we imply that he eventually must appear and provide his services; otherwise he could not possibly profit from their increased value. This implication is certainly valid in connection with most server-client relationships; but it does not flow from the most pronounced form of the histrionics of scarcity: when, in the face of the most intense anticipation, the server never appears! The sense of awe thereby occasioned, moreover, is perhaps most poignant when the server himself is unknown to his attendant, for what then emerges is the unadulterated sense of anticipation itself, uncontaminated by any personal reference. Such is the case of Godot (Beckett 1954), whose efficacy lies in no concrete, substantive achievement but in the pure fact that he is waited for.

Delay and the maintenance of status boundaries. This radical case points up the two contradictory tendencies that are common to the standpoints of all servers: (1) the desire to enter at once into relations with others for "instrumental" reasons and (2) the impulse to hold oneself apart from them for "expressive" ones. This dilemma has a structural as well as a psychological referent. We know that the maintenance and purposes of social organizations require social contact not only among constituents of a single stratum but also between members of different (higher and lower) strata. This prerequisite poses a problem because interpersonal contacts between strata tend in diverse ways to undermine the distance and erode the barriers that distinguish them. Dedifferentiating tendencies of this sort could only redound to the disadvantage of the superior, who profits both materially and morally in proportion to the decisiveness of the separation. The delaying ritual of waiting helps resolve this dilemma. Although the status gap must be bridged by social contact, the contact itself can be depersonalized and formalized; it can be made "by appointment only." This practice follows status lines in a very clear-cut way. While the factory worker, for instance, may approach his peers or even his foreman without appointment, he cannot do so if he is to meet with an executive. The subordinate must be delayed before he is allowed to make a cross-stratal contact. Such inconvenience nicely preserves the sense in which the superior is symbolically inaccessible to those beneath him. While an interactional breach of status boundaries may occur, it can be ritualized in a way which makes it appear that it does not.

The Imposition of Waiting as an Aggressive Act

If the temporal aspect of relationships between those occupying different social positions may be stated in terms of who waits for whom, then we would expect to find a reversal of the waiting-delaying pattern when persons "switch" positions. Furthermore, this reversal may be accentuated through retaliation by the one who suffered under the initial arrangement. A former president furnishes us with an example:

Ken Hechler, who was director of research at the White House from 1948 to 1952, recalled the day Mr. Truman kept Winthrop Aldrich, president of the Chase Manhattan Bank, waiting outside the White House office for 30 minutes. Hechler quoted Mr. Truman as saying:
"When I was a United States senator and headed the war

investigation committee, I had to go to New York to see this fella Aldrich. Even though I had an appointment he had me cool my heels for an hour and a half. So just relax. He's got a little while to go yet."   (*Chicago Daily News*, December 27, 1972: 4)

Punitive sanctioning through the imposition of waiting is met in its most extreme forms when a person is not only kept waiting but is also kept ignorant as to how long he must wait, or even of what he is waiting for. One manifestation of the latter form is depicted by Solzhenitsyn (1968a: 222):

Having met the man (or telephoned him or even specially summoned him), he might say: "Please step into my office tomorrow morning at ten." "Can't I drop in now?" the individual would be sure to ask, since he would be eager to know what he was being summoned for and to get it over with. "No, not now," Rusanov would gently, but strictly admonish. He would not say that he was busy at the moment or had to go to a conference. He would on no account offer a clear, simple reason, something that could reassure the man being summoned (for that was the crux of this device). He would pronounce the words "not now" in a tone allowing many interpretations—not all of them favorable. "About what?" the employee might ask, out of boldness or inexperience. "You'll find out tomorrow," Pavel Nikolaevich would answer in a velvet voice, bypassing the tactless question. But what a long time it is until tomorrow.

The underlying technique for the aggressive use of delay involves the withdrawal or withholding of one's presence with a view to forcing another into an interactionally precarious state wherein he might confront, recognize, and flounder in his own vulnerability or unworthiness.[9] By such means, the superordinate not only affirms his ascendency but does so at the direct expense of his inferior's dignity. Russian bureaucrats are masters at invoking this routine in their dealings with waiting clients:

Casting a disapproving eye at the janitor's wet overshoes, and looking at him severely, Shikin let him stand there while he sat down in an armchair and silently looked over various papers. From time to time, as if he was astonished by what he was reading . . . , he looked up at him in amazement, as one might look at a man-eating beast that has finally been caged. All this was done according to the system and was meant to have an annihilating effect on the prisoner's psyche. A half-hour passed in the locked office in inviolate silence. The lunch bell rang out clearly. Spiridon hoped to receive his letter from home, but Shikin did not even hear the bell; he riffled silently through thick files, he took something out of a box and put it in another box, he leafed, frowning, through various papers and again glanced up briefly in surprise at the dispirited, guilty Spiridon.

All the water from Spiridon's overshoes had dripped on the rubber runner, and they had dried when Shikin finally spoke: "All right, move closer!"   (Solzhenitsyn 1968b: 482–83)

This kind of strategy can only be employed by superordinates who have power over a client in the first place. The effect on the client is to further subordinate him, regardless of a server's initial attractiveness or a client's realization that the delay has been deliberately imposed. Furthermore, this practice leaves the client in a psychologically as well as ritually unsatisfactory state. The two presumably act back on each other in a mutually subversive way, for by causing his client to become tense or nervous the server undermines the self-confidence necessary for him to maintain proper composure. This tendency, incidentally, is routinely applied by skillful police interrogators who deliberately ignore a suspect waiting to be questioned, assuming that a long, uncertain wait will "rattle him" sufficiently to disorganize the kinds of defenses he could use to protect himself (Arthur and Caputo 1959: 31).

Ritual Waiting and Autonomy

We have tried to show that while servers may cause others to wait in order to devote their attention to other necessary matters, they may also make people wait for the pure joy of dramatizing their capacity to do so. Such elation, we saw, is understandable, for by effecting a wait the server demonstrates that his presence is not subject to the disposition or whim of another and that access to him is a privilege not to be taken lightly. And, if access is a privilege, then one may sanction another by deliberately holding oneself apart from him. But we must now make explicit a point that was only implied in our previous discussions: that the imposition of waiting expresses and sustains the autonomy as well as the superiority of the self.

While the imposition of delay allows a superordinate to give expression to his authority, waiting may also be imposed in protest against that authority. The latter achievement is valued, naturally, among those of despised status and low rank. Because they lack the wherewithal to do so in most of their other relations, the powerless, in their capacity as servers, delight in keeping their superiors waiting. The deliberately sluggish movements of many store clerks, telephone operators, cashiers, toll collectors, and the like, testify to the ability of the lowly as well as the lofty to dramatize their autonomy. This accords with Meerloo's (1966: 249) assertion that "the strategy of delay is an ambivalent attack on those who command us." This kind of aggression is perhaps most pronounced under sociologically ambivalent conditions: as the legitimacy of the existing distribution of status honor ceases to be taken for granted, prescribed deference patterns give way to institutionalized rudeness, which may be expressed by appearing late for appointments with a superordinate as well as by dillydallying while he waits for his needs to be served.

It goes without saying that members of the dominant classes are not above such invidious intention. Often having the means to do so, they merely execute it in a diametrically opposite manner: by compulsively refusing to wait. These are the people who are targets of advertising campaigns through which establishments of various sorts announce that their customers do not wait as long as those who shop in lower-priced competitor stores. General store chains (specializing in groceries) have run such ads in the recent past. That time may be a marketable commodity is also confirmed by the frequency with which we observe "No Waiting" signs in the front windows of barber shops. Similarly, those who object to waiting as a matter of principle find satisfaction in "instant-on" television sets, Polaroid photographs, and so forth. For many persons, the higher cost of using such services is offset by the personal sense of self-worth and autonomy thereby affirmed. By paying a higher price, the individual may back up his claim that he is "not the kind of person who will be kept waiting." It needs to be stressed that the inflated price he pays is instrumental to this act of self-affirmation: the value of his time and, therefore, his self, is enhanced precisely because another value is sacrificed on its behalf; the individual thus convinces himself, and perhaps others, that he easily pays a cash price for the opportunity to dispose of it as he wishes. He presumably has "better things to do with his time" than to expend it behind a queue of others (whose time and selves—because they are willing to wait—may not be as valuable as his own).

Ceremonial Waiting

Because unwillingness to wait embodies a rejection of both the auspices under which it is demanded and the inferior self that awaits the incumbent of the waiting role, it may be said that readiness to wait symbolizes a measure of deference toward the authority who imposes it. Those who are kept waiting beyond the appointed time by very high political or professional figures, for instance, may not exhibit indignation or sullenness at being delayed; on the contrary, the client must exhibit gratitude that an audience is granted at all. Thus, the waiting period that is taken in stride by the client of an internationally applauded brain specialist would give rise to seething if inflicted by the neighborhood dentist.

This variation in waiter irritation is governed by a general rule: the more pronounced the honor of the server, the longer we are expected to willingly wait for him. One of the clearest instances of this rule is found in those colleges which have "more or less unofficially standardized periods that students are to await a tardy teacher, and in some instances the period is graded according to the teacher's rank" (Moore 1963: 53).

If readiness to wait with good grace conveys an individual's deference to a person more elevated than himself, we should not be surprised to find an inferior waiting for the very purpose of expressing deference. This form is perhaps most conspicuous in its collective expression. On a very cold day in 1963, for example, almost 250,000 people waited up to 10 hours outside the Capitol Rotunda, where President Kennedy lay in state. Such a massive collective deference gesture can be made intelligible by reference to a simple principle. Given the charisma of its object, an event may be so awe inspiring as to render banal and irrelevant—even profane—whatever one might oneself do. One consequently measures up to the occasion by doing nothing at all. Moreover, because suspension of activity in deference to another entails forfeiture of alternative activities and associated rewards, deferential waiting comes sharply into view as a functional equivalent to sacrifice. When in addition the renunciatory deferential tribute is rendered in proximity to a sacred center, its personal meaning is naturally intensified and focused. As one member of the long queue leading to the Capitol Rotunda put it: "We were going to watch it on television in our room at the 'Y.' But the more we watched the more we felt we just had to do something—something" (*New York Times*, November 25, 1963: 5). To wait deferentially at a sacred center is thus to be "where the action is," or, more precisely, where the in-action is.

The respect pattern. The above is simply an extraordinary expression of the mundane tendency for persons to subject themselves to a wait as a sign of deference for those with whom they have an engagement. Hall (1959: 18) refers to this as "the respect pattern" which inclines persons to arrive a little early for meetings and rendezvous so as not to subject another or others to such inconvenience and abasement as has been herein described. Self-imposed waiting is governed by the same rule that regulates the impatience of those on whom waiting is imposed by another: the higher the rank of that other, the more imperative an unambiguous demonstration of the respect pattern becomes. For example, White House etiquette (as enunciated by Emily Post [1965: 48]) dictates that: "When you are invited to The White House, you must arrive several minutes, at least, before the hour specified. No more unforgiveable breach of etiquette can be made than not to be standing in the drawing room when the President makes his entry." One of the most radical modes of this kind of ceremonial waiting was found in the Ethiopian practice of "Studying the Gate."[10] This involved a procedure followed by those who desired an audience with the emperor, for whose sake callers arrived several hours before their appointment and waited patiently outside the door leading to his chamber. Thus situated, visitors exhibited their respect, subjects their devotion, to him.

Individuals may express deference not only by arriving early and waiting for the appearance of a distinguished person, they may also wait for the departure of that person before leaving themselves. For some occasions this possibility becomes an imperative. Thus, according to Fenwick (1948: 469), "The two cardinal points of White House Etiquette are that no guest is late and that no guest leaves before the President and his wife have gone upstairs." This rule shows that just as waiting may ritually precede access to another it may also precede his departure. A most radical example of the latter is the phenomenon of the death vigil, wherein a group awaits news of the passing of a prominent member and disperses when it is received. This form stands as a functional parallel to waiting for an honored person to depart before leaving oneself.

When juxtaposed with our initial remarks, such considerations as these (as well as others introduced in this paper) admit of a typological possibility that deserves more singular attention than it has up to now received.

Instrumental waiting and ceremonial waiting. It is possible to distribute empirical instances across a continuum limited at one end by purely instrumental waiting, necessitated by the server's interactional inaccessibility due to real demands on his time and energy. Between the poles of this continuum we find cases which present the difficulty of ascertaining to what extent the wait may, on the one hand, be occasioned by the server's objective scarcity and, on the other, by the demand for temporal tribute implied in his refusal to open himself up for interaction at the first available instant.[11] Perhaps most cases would fall into this middle category, for, as Shils (1970: 433) suggests, "Deference actions are not . . . always massive actions of much duration. They occur moreover mainly at the margin of other types of action. . . . Between beginning and end, deference actions are performed in fusion with non-deferential actions." However, we have observed deferential waiting in far less attenuated, far purer (indeed ceremonial) forms. These constitute the limit of the other end of the continuum to which we are referring.

As an extreme case, ceremonial waiting sets in relief the devaluating aspects of waiting in more ordinary contexts. Precisely because it exaggerates their degradational implications, ceremonial waiting permits us to analyze these less radical forms in terms of their ritual "distancing" or "boundary maintenance" functions, through which superordinates may dramatize and so confirm their position in the social structure. However, we must not forget that the superordinate may be challenged by the very same means through which he confirms himself. We have ourselves observed compulsive refusals to wait. In view of this, we must concede that ritualized status-elevational possibilities—or, at least, reaffirmational ones—exist on both sides of the server-waiter relationship.

Summary

Delay is a relevant sociological datum because it is general throughout society, is a measure of access to goods and services, and indexes the efficiency of the organizations which distribute them. Above all, delay entails two kinds of very conspicuous costs. Having nothing to do with waiting as such but rather with the losses occasioned by it, value foregone through idleness is an extrinsic disadvantage. On the other hand, the degradational implications of being kept idle are intrinsic to waiting and can arise in no way other than through involuntary delay. The purpose of this paper was to explore the way these costs are distributed throughout the social structure and to identify the principles to which this allocation gives expression.

We have introduced the category of power, as exercised in server-client relationships, as the ultimate determinant of delay, the main assertion being that the distribution of waiting time coincides with the distribution of power. This proposition turns on the assumption that power is related to the scarcity of goods and skills that an individual server possesses. Accordingly, the relationship between servers and clients in respect to waiting is an instance of an "organized dependency relationship" (Stinchcombe 1970): servers' holding power is contingent upon clients not being able to frequent less accessible and/or more expensive servers, while client autonomy requires their availability. Delay is therefore longest when the client is more dependent on the relationship than the server; it is minimized, however, when the server is the overcommitted member of an asymmetrical relationship.[12] Personal and structural factors thus stand as intersecting contingencies: resourceful persons wait less within both competitive and monopolistic markets, while delay will be more pronounced in the latter regardless of personal power.

If waiting is related to a person's position in a power network, then a server may confirm or enhance his status by deliberately making another wait for him. In a more general sense, this is to say that the management of availability itself, regardless of the purpose for which an individual makes himself available, carries with it distinct psychological implications. Because a person's access to others indexes his scarcity as a social object, that person's social worth may only be realized by demonstrated inaccessibility. Openness to social relations may therefore be restricted not only to regulate interactional demands but also to enhance the self that one brings to an interaction. Because it is independent of the objective scarcity of servers and their resources, this type of delay was subsumed under the category of "ritual waiting." This form finds expression in positive as well as negative respects: just as a server may deliberately limit access to himself, so a client may wait when it is circumstantially unnecessary in order to exhibit deference to a server. The initial relationship between waiting and power thus gives rise to processes which strengthen it. That is to say, secondary dramaturgical modes have come to subserve a fact that was originally grounded in an objective supply-demand structure.

The broader implication of this essay is that it finds in time itself a generalized resource whose distribution affects life chances with regard to the attainment of other, more specific kinds of rewards. This is true in a number of respects. Time, like money, is valuable because it is necessary for the achievement of productive purposes; ends cannot be reached unless an appropriate amount of it is "spent" or "invested" on their behalf. On the other hand, the power that a time surplus makes possible may be protected and/or expanded by depriving others of their time. By creating queues to reduce idle periods, for example, a server exploits clients by converting their time to his own use. A server does the same by "overcharging" in the sense of deliberately causing a particular client to wait longer than necessary.

The monetary analogies we have used are not without some justification. Just as money possesses no substantive value independent of its use as a means of exchange, time can only be of value if put to substantive use in some kind of an exchange relationship. Both time and money may be regarded as generalized means because both are possessed in finite quantities; both may be counted, saved, spent, lost, wasted, or invested. And, just as the budget (which, for Weber [1964: 187], is the highest form of economic rationality) "states systematically in what way the means which are expected to be used within the unit for an accounting period ... can be covered by the anticipated income," so the time schedule—which may be the highest form of interactional rationality—states in an identical way how the time required for the performance of numerous activities can be covered by its anticipated availability. Accordingly, while the powerful can allocate monetary means to their own desired ends by controlling the budget, they also regulate the distribution of time—rewarding themselves, depriving others—through their control of the schedule. What is at stake in the first instance is the amount of resources to which different parts of a system are entitled; in the second, it is the priority of their entitlements. Far from being a coincidental byproduct of power, then, control of time comes into view as one of its essential properties.

2   Emergency Department Structure and Waiting Time

Organizations have limited amounts of resources with which to dispense goods or administer services. For this reason, some measure of client waiting is inevitable. The elimination of queues would require, after all, that servers continually outnumber clients; but this ratio would make their services prohibitively expensive. Queuing is therefore a fundamental property of all organizations which process people. However, there is much variation in the waiting times associated with such organizations. The purpose of this chapter is to investigate these differences in one group of medical emergency departments.

The speed with which a medical system can serve its patients is important for a number of reasons. First of all, an involuntary delay causes a client to renounce more rewarding investments of his time, which is no small sacrifice. For example, in a recent national survey (Andersen 1971: 46–47) waiting time in doctors' offices and clinics was reported to be one of the major sources of dissatisfaction with medical care. These data also suggested that a high level of dissatisfaction is related less to such intrinsic aspects of waiting as boredom than to its extrinsic costs, expressed in terms of other activities foregone through idleness.

Waiting time is also important because it measures access to medical care. Although we are accustomed to thinking of the accessibility of a service in geographical and monetary terms, we need to recognize that this concept subsumes any extramotivational factor which represents a barrier to consumption. Far more than we realize, delay performs such a function. It is known that the many patients who abandon a queue before treatment do so because of long waiting periods.[1] And it is widely held that many patients are discouraged from even seeking medical care because of the prospect of unacceptably long delays. This contingency has in some cases even led to fatal consequences.[2] We therefore need to be careful in assuming impatience to be the only consequence of delay. For some, inordinate amounts of waiting time make medical service unattainable.

Waiting time in medical settings is worth investigating for yet another reason. Because the cost an organization incurs in providing service is constant at any point in time, the rate at which it can process clients may be taken as at least one index of its efficiency (Gibson, Anderson, and Bugbee 1970: 202). Given two or more emergency rooms which serve identical numbers and kinds of patients with equal effectiveness, and which in so doing incur identical costs, the one which administers to clients at the fastest rate is to be considered the most efficient. The element of efficiency is of course most crucial in competitive organizations, where the short queue is a selling point. This is less true of medical systems, where "shopping around" is frowned upon and sometimes impossible. Nevertheless, the efficiency of these systems is highly consequential with respect to *client* costs, whether these be expressed on an individual or aggregate level.

The Problem

In this investigation we seek to identify some of the factors which augment or diminish waiting time in medical emergency departments and to explore the broader sociological principles to which these observable effects relate. We bring to this problem two basic assumptions. The first is that waiting time is associated with the relations of supply and demand. When the number of clients arriving during some time interval exceeds the number which can be served, waiting time will be longer than when the service rate exceeds the arrival rate. Our second assumption relates to the organization of service. While increases in staffing enhance the productivity of an organization, they also complicate its structure. This is because the organization of service becomes more differentiated as the number of personnel is increased. Differentiation in emergency departments occurs along at least two lines: (1) larger staffs tend to be more heterogeneous in terms of the number of medical and auxiliary specialties represented in them, and (2) larger staffs must be accommodated by a more differentiated spatial area.

Both forms of differentiation admit of advantages. Specialized work is typically carried out more efficiently and greater numbers of treatment rooms enable an organization to care for more patients simultaneously. But at the same time differentiation complicates the necessary functions of communication and coordination, and this difficulty adversely affects its processing rate.

Waiting time is thus an outcome of the organization as well as the quantity of service. In more formal words, queuing phenomena may be understood in terms of a "scarcity model," which directs attention exclusively to the relative quantities of supply and demand, and a "structural model," which highlights the organization of service, independently of supply-demand contingencies. This distinction raises three empirical questions, to which there are presently no answers:

1. What are the relative effects on waiting time of the supply-demand relation, on the one hand, and the structure of the emergency room on the other? That is, which formulation — the "scarcity model" or the "structural model" — has the most explanatory value?

2. If we confine ourselves to variation in organizational modes, will we find that increased differentiation on balance promotes or diminishes emergency department waiting time?

3. Are the effects of supply-demand and organizational contingencies invariant with respect to one another or must their interaction be taken into account to fully realize these effects?

Data Collection

The materials on which this investigation is based were gathered in connection with the Chicago Survey on Emergency Medical Services conducted by the Center for Health Administration Studies of the University of Chicago (see Gibson, Anderson, and Bugbee 1970).

Beginning October 1, 1968, on-site surveys were made by study teams at 78 of 80 hospitals in Cook County, Illinois. In addition to material collected from hospital files, administrators and supervisory staff of each hospital were interviewed. Each patient was also followed through the processing routine, from the time of his admission to time of discharge, during a 24-hour period in the emergency departments of 70 of the 80 hospitals.

To ensure some measure of temporal representation, ten

emergency departments, randomly selected, were visited for each day of the week (though not all ten units were observed on the same date). The typical procedure was for a department to be covered by two twelve-hour shifts beginning and ending at 8 a.m. This phase of the project began in June 1969 and lasted until the following spring, although about half of the 70 units were observed during the first four months of data collection. What we have, then, is a predominantly summer-early fall sample. The sample itself consisted of 2,808 patients visiting the 69 emergency departments for which complete data were available. The unit of analysis for this investigation is the emergency department.

Measurement

Our objectives require estimates of emergency department waiting time, daily arrivals, staffing, division of labor, and spatial differentiation. These dimensions were measured with suitable degrees of accuracy.

Waiting time is defined as the interval between the moment a patient is formally admitted to an emergency department by a nurse or registration clerk and the time he is seen by a doctor. This datum was directly recorded by the on-site observer. An emergency department's waiting time is defined as the median waiting time of all patients who were admitted by it on the day it was observed. This variable is dichotomized at 15 minutes, which is somewhat below the median of 17.6 minutes.[3]

Daily arrivals simply refers to the number of persons admitted by an emergency department on the day it was observed. The 69 arrival volumes are dichotomized between 39 and 40.

The *staffing* of an emergency room was computed from duty schedules and involves an average of the number of morning, evening, and night personnel. This variable was dichotomized between 3.59 and 3.60.

Staff differentiation in an emergency room is the number of occupational specialties represented within it. The categories include physicians, residents, interns, registered nurses, practical nurses, aides and orderlies. This index is dichotomized at three occupational categories.

Finally, *spatial differentiation* refers to the maximum number of rooms within an emergency department which can be used for the purpose of treatment. Information on this variable was obtained from the space allocation section of the forms completed through interviews of emergency department administrators. The specific item calls for information as to the "number of patients the emergency department is designed to treat simultaneously." This distribution is dichotomized between 5 and 6.

It is this last variable which perhaps poses the most sticky conceptual problem. It may be said with some justification that the sheer number of separate rooms or treatment areas is a measure of size, not differentiation. In the sense that additional areas increase processing capacity, this objection may be well taken. However, the division of space reproduces the functions of operational differentiation in that it places constraints upon communication and intensifies the problem of coordinating activities. For this reason we have subsumed the mere partitioning of space under the sociological category of differentiation, whose basic referents, after all, are of an *interactional* nature.

Results

As will be seen, the independent variables are highly associated with one another. Emergency departments which accommodate the most patients tend to have not only the largest and most differentiated staffs but also the most spatial differentiation. However, the larger and smaller departments are fairly comparable with respect to patient characteristics, both medical and social;[4] as such, these characteristics cannot be used to explain waiting time differences among them.

Waiting Time and the Relations of Supply and Demand

If an emergency department's waiting time reflects the ratio of the size of its staff to the number of patients making demands upon it, then we would expect to find independent effects for both variables. Increasing the number of daily arrivals should increase waiting time if staff size is held constant; but if staffing is increased while arrivals are controlled, delay and congestion should be reduced. The real situation is not that simple, however.

If we look first at the column totals in table 1, we find that 47

TABLE 1.   Percentage of Emergency Departments with Long
Waiting Times (by Daily Patient Arrivals and Staff
Size)

Staff Size[a]	Number of Daily Arrivals[b]		Total
	Low	High	
Small	44(23)	78(9)	53(32)
Large	54(13)	71(24)	65(37)
Total	47(36)	73(33)	59(69)

Note: Number of departments given in parentheses.

[a]A staff is *small* when its average is 3.59 or less; *large*, when
3.60 or more.

[b]Forty or more daily arrivals is *high*; 39 or less is *low*.

percent of the emergency departments with a low number of
daily arrivals have a mean patient waiting time of 15 minutes or
more. Among departments with a high number of arrivals the
corresponding percentage is 73. The greater the number of
patients admitted, the longer the waiting time. The direction of
this relationship is the same regardless of the size of the
department staff. Looking next to the row totals in table 1, we
observe the highest probability of *long* waiting times among the
emergency departments which are best staffed (65 as opposed
to 53 percent). However, this picture changes somewhat when
patient demand is held constant. Among organizations with the
fewest arrivals, long waiting times are found in 44 percent of
those with small staffs and 54 percent of those with large
staffs—a difference of 10 percentage points. The direction of
this relationship is reversed in the units with the most arrivals,
where long waits are decreased by 7 percent among departments with large staffs.

That generous staffing should decrease the waiting times of
the most inundated facilities but produce increases in all others
is a conclusion that we would be hard-pressed to draw from
these weak associations. The safest thing to say at this point is
that when patient volume is controlled, staffing exerts no effects
on emergency department waiting time.[5] Whether or not a true
inverse relationship between staffing and waiting time is being
concealed by some other variable remains to be seen.

We can say now, however, that the effects just observed, and
those which we are about to observe, are independent of mean

department treatment time. This was unambiguously demonstrated in a separate analysis.[6]

Waiting Time and the Organization of Service

The assumption that waiting time is a direct consequence of the simple relations of supply and demand has only been partly confirmed and we are left with the puzzling fact that increments in department staffing do not substantially reduce delay, even when patient demand is held constant. By turning to the social organization of the emergency room, however, we can pose a number of fresh problems and in so doing address this dilemma in an indirect way.

Staff Differentiation and Waiting Time. Increase in the size of an organization brings about a more refined division of labor (Blau 1970). This is an empirical generalization which is highly descriptive of Cook County emergency departments. Whether we take as our index of size the volume of patient demand or staffing, we find a direct association between department size and number of occupational categories (see table 2).

TABLE 2.   Percentage of Emergency Departments with Long Waiting Times (by Daily Patient Arrivals, Staff Size, and Staff Differentiation)

Staff Differentiation[a]	Number of Daily Arrivals		Totals
	Low	High	
Small Staff Size			
Low	44(16)	100(5)	57(21)
High	43(7)	50(4)	46(11)
Total	44(23)	78(9)	53(32)
Large Staff Size			
Low	50(4)	100(5)	78(9)
High	56(9)	63(19)	61(28)
Total	54(13)	71(24)	65(37)
Totals			
Low	45(20)	100(10)	64(30)
High	50(16)	61(23)	56(39)
Total	47(36)	73(33)	59(69)

[a]A staff's differentiation is *low* when the number of occupational categories represented in it is three or less; *high* when there are four or more categories.

The larger emergency departments are faced with special problems. Besides their main function of administering medical service, these organizations must process large numbers of often impatient clients in an orderly fashion and, at the same time, keep a written account of their many transactions with them. Task differentiation promotes efficiency in this respect because it allows each staff member to concentrate on a limited sphere of work. Part of the emergency room personnel may thus devote themselves exclusively to medical tasks while the other part satisfies the imperatives of social and administrative order. That such an arrangement promotes efficiency by reducing waiting time is confirmed in table 2.

The lower right-hand corner of table 2 discloses that 64 percent of the emergency departments with three or less occupational specialties show mean waiting times of 15 minutes or more; for those with four or more specialties, the long wait index is 56 percent. The direction of this association is not only maintained but also strengthened when staff size (with which staff differentiation is highly correlated) is held constant. For small staffs, high differentiation reduces the long wait percentage from 57 to 46 percent; for large staffs, the reduction is from 78 to 61 percent.

Staff differentiation is also associated with number of arrivals. When this factor is brought under control a differential relationship emerges. The bottom (column) totals of the table show that staff differentiation does not reduce waiting times among the smaller, less inundated departments. For the large departments, however, there is a substantial reduction. One hundred percent of the largest and least differentiated departments show long waiting times, as opposed to 61 percent of the largest and most differentiated emergency units. In other words, it is only among the inundated emergency rooms with large-scale operations that an advanced division of labor brings about reductions in waiting time. Moreover, table 2 demonstrates that this principle is unaffected by the absolute size of the staffs in these organizations.

Staff differentiation not only affects waiting time directly; it also modifies the impact of other variables. Looking once again to the totals at the bottom of table 2, but this time reading across, we find the effect of patient demand on waiting time to be far more pronounced in the least differentiated departments. Among these, 45 percent of the units with a low number of arrivals have long waiting times, compared to 100 percent of those with a high number—a difference of 55 percentage points. The comparable percentages for the emergency rooms with high staff differentiation are 50 and 61, a difference of only 11 points. This pattern maintains itself regardless of the size of staff, as the body of table 2 plainly shows. Efficiencies created by pronounced differentiation thus facilitate patient processing by minimizing the effect of client demand.

Long waiting periods are most likely to be found in the most inundated and least differentiated facilities. Either an increase in differentiation or a decrease in patient volume tends to reduce waiting time, but the occurrence of both does not reduce it further. This is true regardless of staff size. Thus, a low number of patients reduces delay; but it also negates the advantage that staff differentiation would otherwise have. The reason for this, perhaps, is that a division of labor will only produce economies in operations when the level of demand is high enough to keep staff members continually busy at specialized tasks. If patient demand is not heavy, then one person can perform a variety of functions and a pronounced division of labor becomes functionally superfluous.

One final result may be drawn from table 2. Neither staff differentiation alone nor its interaction with patient demand alters the effect of staff size, which, if anything, tends now to almost consistently *increase* waiting time—an anomaly which will be presently explained.

*Spatial Differentiation and Waiting Time.*The greater the number of arrivals an emergency department must accommodate, the more treatment rooms it must provide for staff to work in and the more patients it can process simultaneously. It would therefore seem that, with everything else constant, departments with the most treatment areas would have the shortest waiting times. It turns out that just the opposite is the case.

Table 3 shows that, overall, 41 percent of the departments with low spatial differentiation produce long waiting times, as opposed to 83 percent of the departments with high differentiation. The direction of this relationship is maintained regard-

TABLE 3.   Percentage of Emergency Departments with Long Waiting Times (by Daily Patient Arrivals, Staff Size, and Spatial Differentiation)

Spatial Differentiation[a]	Number of Daily Arrivals		Totals
	Low	High	
Small Staff Size			
Low	38(21)	67(6)	44(27)
High	100(2)	100(3)	100(5)
Total	44(23)	78(9)	53(32)
Large Staff Size			
Low	20(5)	43(7)	33(12)
High	75(8)	82(17)	80(25)
Total	54(13)	71(24)	65(37)
Totals			
Low	35(26)	54(13)	41(39)
High	80(10)	85(20)	83(30)
Total	47(36)	73(33)	59(69)

[a]Spatial differentiation is *high* when six or more rooms within the emergency department may be used for examination and treatment; it is *low* when five rooms or less may be used.

less of the size of department staff (see row totals) and regardless of the number of daily arrivals (see column totals). The body of the table shows that the direction of the relationship is unaffected when staffing and arrivals are controlled simultaneously.

However, the effect on waiting time of patient volume is greatest in the departments with the smallest number of treatment rooms. Reading across the totals at the bottom of table 3, we find that a high number of arrivals increases long waits by 19 percent in departments with the fewest treatment rooms and by only 5 percent in departments with the most rooms. Although no increase in long waits is possible in highly differentiated departments with small staffs (the low arrival percentage being 100), highly differentiated facilities with large staffs show only a 7-point increase. In departments with the least spatial differentiation, however, the corresponding percentage point increases in long waits are 29 and 23. The spatial differentiation of an emergency department thus seems to produce paradoxical effects on the efficiency of its operations. On the one hand, more working areas directly lengthen waiting time. But when patient demand is increased, larger numbers of treatment rooms tend to reduce its effect on delay.

The relationship between staffing and waiting time is another fact to which we may turn our attention. If we look at the row totals in table 3, we will find that generous staffing increases the probability of long waits (from 53 to 65 percent). But these same totals show that when we vary staff size and control for spatial complexity, increases in staff invariably reduce waiting time, as we originally expected them to do. In emergency departments with the most rudimentary division of space, increased staffing reduces the probability of long waits from 44 to 33 percent; for those with the most advanced division, the reduction is from 100 to 80 percent. The direction of this relationship maintains itself and its magnitude is generally increased when number of arrivals and spatial differentiation are controlled simultaneously, as the body of table 3 shows.

These findings mean that number of staff and number of separate treatment areas are acting as "suppressor variables" with respect to one another. This is because they are directly associated but correlated with waiting time in opposite directions, with spatial capacity having an independent positive effect, and, staffing, an independent negative effect. Because the latter influence is the weaker, it is masked when the former is allowed to vary. The control of one of the above variables thus *increases* the association of the other with waiting time.

While these data are not longitudinal, they do seem to suggest that increases in patient demand tend to bring about increases in staff, which meets that demand and reduces its effect on waiting time. However, larger staff size coincides with spatial differentiation, which overcomes its advantageous effects by reducing efficiency of operations and increasing waiting time. But we are now faced with a puzzling problem. If the size of its staff is coordinated mainly with the demand made on an emergency facility (or vice-versa, for that matter), why is it that spatial differentiation, rather than demand itself, masks the true influence of staffing? After all, is spatial differentiation not merely an instrumental by-product of meeting patient demand: The answer to this question is emphatically, "No." An internal analysis of table 3 will show that spatial differentiation and staff size exhibit considerable covariation even when number of arrivals is held constant.[7] This is to say that emergency facilities are expanded to accommodate a growing staff, or that staff are added to fill up existing space, regardless of the amount of work to be done.

These findings may help to explain why increased differentiation of space within an emergency department should in and of itself lengthen waiting time, regardless of variations in supply and demand. We know that the spatial structure of departments becomes more complex with increases in the absolute level of medical service. And we suspect that extensive subdivision of space intensifies problems of communication and coordination, which create new social demands whose satisfaction can only diminish the amount of time normally devoted to patients. The very means through which emergency departments facilitate the handling of patients may therefore create problems which subvert this process. Perhaps the condition under which the costs of spatial expansion exceed its benefits is when the addition of space, independently of the addition of servers, is used to meet patient needs. This is the case in the present data. Another internal analysis of table 3 shows that the extent of a department's division of space is as good an independent predictor of the volume of patients as is the size of its staff.[8] This means that staffing does not mediate the relationship between client demand and space. But rooms themselves, independently of servers, do not contribute to the processing of clients; their independent increase, therefore, can only add costs to a processing system—expressed in terms of communicational complexities and the resulting time withdrawn from treatment of patients—without supplying benefits to overcome them. This interpretation is consistent with the row totals in table 3, which show that a pronounced spatial differentiation tends to have a somewhat greater effect on waiting time where staffing is at a minimum.

A Comparison of the Effects of Spatial and Staff Differentiation. The direction of effects on waiting of spatial differentiation (table 3) is very consistent. It remains only to demonstrate their independence of and to explore their relationship to staff differentiation.

Table 4 shows that the direct relationship between spatial differentiation and waiting time maintains itself among high and low levels of staff differentiation. In the former category, 76

TABLE 4.   Percentage of Emergency Departments with Long
             Waiting Times (by Daily Patient Arrivals, Staff
             Differentiation, and Spatial Differentiation)

| Spatial | Number of Daily Arrivals | | |
Differentiation	Low	High	Totals
Low staff differentiation			
Low	35(17)	100(4)	48(21)
High	100(3)	100(6)	100(9)
Total	45(20)	100(10)	63(30)
High staff differentiation			
Low	33(9)	33(9)	33(18)
High	72(7)	78(14)	76(21)
Total	50(16)	61(23)	56(39)
Totals			
Low	35(26)	54(13)	41(39)
High	80(10)	85(20)	83(30)
Total	47(36)	73(33)	59(69)

percent of the departments with a high number of treatment
rooms produce long waiting times, as opposed to 33 percent of
the departments with a smaller spatial capacity. Corresponding
percentages for a low level of staff specialization are 100 and 48
(see row totals). The direction of this relationship tends to be
maintained when arrival and specialties are simultaneously
controlled, with one exception: where large numbers of arrivals
intersect with a low degree of staff differentiation the influence
of spatial capacity is negated. Table 4 also shows that the
inverse relationship between staff differentiation and waiting
time is maintained regardless of whether the spatial factor is
controlled separately or in combination with number of arrivals.
(A separate analysis shows this pattern to be unaffected when
staffing is substituted, as a control, for volume.)

Finally, spatial and staff differentiation modify the effect of
arrival volume on waiting time in a very striking way. Looking at
the body of the table we find that, while there is no room for
increase in percentage of long waits among departments with
high spatial and low staff differentiation, it is clear that arrival
volume has little effect on delay among departments with
highly differentiated staffs. Within this category, the percentage
differences derived from a comparison of high and low numbers

of arrivals are six for departments with high spatial capacity and zero for departments of low capacity. Only when an emergency department is relatively undifferentiated with respect to *both* staffing and its physical space will arrivals accumulate and lengthen department waiting time. (The percentage difference is 65.) This finding seems to justify the conclusion that any form of differentiation heightens the capacity of an emergency treatment system to process its clients.

Summary

The data we have analyzed show quite unambiguously that waiting time in medical organizations cannot be derived from a simple linear combination of other properties of these organizations. The effect of any one independent variable differs considerably according to the level (or combinations thereof) of the other independent variables under which it is "activated." The strongest and weakest relationships thus appear in the simplest and higher order interactions. Because the basic objective of this investigation was to assess the relative power of the "scarcity" and "organizational models" of delay, the discovery of complex interaction effects creates problems of inference, for the influence of client demand is more pronounced under some organizational conditions than others; similarly, the impact of organizational variations differs at varying levels of demand. In addition, the theoretical realms of "scarcity" and "organization" are both indexed by two variables, each of which displays unique patterns of association with waiting time.

At this point, then, we still have no overall assessment of the relative effects of supply-demand relations and social organization. We decided to obtain such a measure by combining the four separate indices into two variables, weighting each index in terms of the direction of its independent association with waiting time. Thus, emergency departments with a high number of arrivals and a small staff were found to have the longest waiting time (to which arrivals are directly and, staffing, inversely, correlated). These departments were assigned a value of 3. A value of 1 was assigned to units with the opposite properties (low numbers of arrivals and large staffs). Emergency departments which were high or low in both respects were assigned a value of 2. The same procedure was followed for staff and spatial differentiation, which are inversely and directly associated with waiting time. High spatial and low staff differentiation is represented by a value of 3; low spatial and high staff differentiation is scored as 1; departments which are high and low in both respects are scored 2.

These two contrived variables were brought together with a view to determining their separate, independent effects on waiting time. The results are displayed in table 5.

We may first compare the row totals. As the ratio between staffing and arrivals becomes less favorable (i.e., as the number of servers in proportion to arrivals shrinks), the probability of long waits increases from 54 through 58 to 78 percent—a percentage difference of 24. Looking now to the column totals, it can be seen that the probability of long waits increases from 33 to 100 percent as we move from the most to the least favorable structures. The percentage difference of 67 percent is almost three times as great as that which obtains for the supply-demand dimension. Furthermore, this difference is unaffected by the level of supply and demand at which it is computed. On the other hand, the effect of the latter is most definitely conditioned by the level of the former. Only in emergency departments which are both high or low in spatial and staff differentiation (departments of intermediate favora-

TABLE 5.   Percentage of Emergency Departments with Long Waiting Times (by Differentiation and Supply-Demand Structures)

Supply-Demand Structure[a]	Differentiation Structure[b]			
	Favorable	Intermediate	Unfavorable	Total
Favorable	33(3)	50(8)	100(2)	54(13)
Intermediate	33(12)	60(30)	100(5)	58(47)
Unfavorable	33(3)	100(4)	100(2)	78(9)
Total	33(18)	62(42)	100(9)	59(69)

[a]The supply-demand structure of an emergency department is favorable when number of arrivals is low and staff is large; intermediate when arrivals and staffing are both either high or low; unfavorable when number of arrivals is high and staff is small.

[b]Emergency departments are favorably differentiated when their staff differentiation is high and their spatial differentiation is low; intermediately differentiated when they are either high or low in both respects; unfavorably differentiated when staff specialization is low and differentiation of space is high.

bility with respect to waiting time) does the supply-demand variable affect long waits, whose probability then increases from 50 through 60 to 100 percent—a difference of 50 points.

Although these two variables were constructed in a most arbitrary manner, which purposely ignores their constituents' relative direct effects on waiting time as well as the interaction effects to which they contribute, they do seem to point to a rather unambiguous conclusion: that the structure of an emergency department is at least as important a determinant of its waiting time as the supply-demand contingencies associated with it.

However, the separate effects attributable to these two conditions should not obscure the dialectical nature of their relationship. Our report has shown that an increase in service for the purpose of meeting client demand brings with it a transformation in the structure of that service, as well as the structure of the facility in which it is offered. These outcomes in turn affect the efficiency with which service is administered: a measure designed to reduce client delay may, through a set of unintended organizational consequences, actually prolong it. The simple supply-demand model is for this reason inadequate for the analysis of delay and congestion; the weakness of the model inheres in its subordination of the fact that service must be organized. We are entitled to draw such a conclusion because the structure of staff organization superimposes itself upon input-output dynamics in an empirically significant way.

3   Manuscript Queues and Editorial Organization

       This chapter examines the processing of manuscripts in the editorial office of a professional journal. The work was undertaken for a number of reasons. Besides its relevance for the problem of how processing systems in general operate and may be improved, an analysis of delay and congestion in the treatment of manuscripts is important in its own right. In context of the current "information explosion," many professional journals are finding themselves unable to keep up with the growing number of papers submitted to them. Distributional means seem therefore to be lagging more and more behind a rising quantity of intellectual production. Because the dissemination of new knowledge and ideas is a key function in the organization of a profession, bottlenecks in the flow of information warrant serious consideration. More specifically, that portion of a profession's pool of new information lying dormant in an editor's or reviewer's work queue represents part of its nonproductive "capital." This is not to mention the costs individual researchers must bear as a result of congestion in editorial systems—particularly among professions in which recognition and advancement are based largely on scholarly publication. A paper can yield no returns of any kind for its author while it lies idle on an editor's or referee's desk.

       The editorial process itself may be viewed as a queuing system whose "clients" or "elements" are the manuscripts submitted by contributing authors. The advantage in subsuming the present problem under such a model inheres in the parameters of the model itself, which raises questions concerning the structured sequence of manuscript processing, the relative contribution of each phase to the total waiting time of an author, how the system's level of input differentially affects its separate queues, and the priorities which govern the order in which manuscripts are treated. The purpose of this investigation is to estimate these parameters and to show how they relate to the internal constraints and dynamics of the editorial process.

Research Setting and Problem

The data on which this investigation is based were furnished by the editor of the *American Journal of Sociology*. As one of the major outlets for sociological information, this journal receives a very large number of documents; however, the number of manhours spent administering to them is quite limited.

Four part-time and two full-time positions make up the journal's staff. The editor, of course, bears ultimate responsibility for the journal's operation and content. He is assisted by a full-time managing editor and assistant whose jobs include overseeing the flow of manuscripts by communicating with referees and authors. Three associate editors recruited from the University of Chicago Sociology Department take part in the assignment of papers to referees and in the final decision on their worthiness for publication. The journal's seventh member, the book review editor, does not participate in these operations, although his work does subtract from the administrative and clerical time available to them.

The processing of a manuscript submitted to the *American Journal of Sociology* follows a typical sequence. As soon as the paper arrives, a face sheet is made out indicating author, title, and date of receipt; it is then placed in a pile of incoming work. This material awaits the meeting of the editorial board (the editor and his associates) which usually takes place every other week. At this conference, the paper is perused or its abstract read, then assigned to two referees. These designations are recorded and the paper is mailed out. When both reviewers have communicated their evaluation, the manuscript is slated for the next meeting of the editorial board. The decision of the board is recorded and the manuscript is placed in a pile of other papers destined to be returned to their authors. In the rare case of an approval without even minor revision, a letter of acceptance is sent to the author after his manuscript has been checked for format and technical or other problems.

The above is a highly schematized version of a manuscript's progress, from which reality departs at several points. For example, service is often expedited by returning a paper immediately after the board decides its content to be inappropriate. Or a manuscript which looks questionable on its face may be reviewed by an associate editor and returned to the author, if the initial impression is confirmed. On the other hand, delays are caused by referees who decline the invitation to read a paper (an act which may take several weeks), after which a fresh reviewer must be designated. Or the staff may discover after two months that a referee who cannot be located is not going to return a paper at all. This contingency adds massive amounts of time to a manuscript's administrative career. In addition, some of those evaluations which arrive in due course are inconsistent or ambiguous, so that a member of the editorial board must read the paper and report his own impressions at a later meeting. As for the task of advising a contributor as to the fate of his paper, this is not always a matter of a short letter. Referees' comments to the author may have to be edited, for any number of reasons. And the board's evaluation must be accurately summarized, especially when a paper is returned for mandatory revision or when an accepted paper is returned with a recommendation for improvements before publication. Many letters, then, require careful and time-consuming composition which can only augment the waiting time of their recipients.

Whatever the complications to which they are subject, four basic and invariant stages may be abstracted from the editing process: (1) the amount of time elapsing between the date a manuscript is received from a contributor and the day it is assigned a referee; (2) referee's reading time; (3) the interval between the day an evaluation is received from the second referee and the day it is given a final disposition; and (4) the time it takes to communicate to the author the board's and referees' evaluation. The editorial process is thus conceived as a "four-station queue": manuscripts must wait to be assigned, read, disposed of, and returned (with good news or bad). This scheme certainly does not account for the total processing time. It excludes delays of papers en route to and from referees and contributors; it does not take into account the fact that sometimes a week may pass between a manuscript's assignment to a referee and the date it is actually sent to him. (There is also a "mail queue.") Nevertheless, this four-step model does encompass the most sizable and important delay intervals.

Our basic problem is twofold: to determine the relative contribution to total processing time of the separate phases of the editorial sequence, and to explain variation in manuscript waiting time within each of these phases. The outcome of such an analysis will enable us to pinpoint the step at which bottlenecks in the processing system occur, identify their causes, and uncover whatever priorities the editorial system resorts to in its attempt to manage an endless flow of manuscripts.

Data Collection and Measurement

In the editorial office of the *American Journal of Sociology* are stored the records of all manuscripts submitted to it during the past four years. A portion of the records for previous years, going back as far as 1966, was also available. These documents were segregated into three groups: (1) rejected papers; (2) papers which had been published or accepted for publication; and (3) papers for which no decision had yet been made. The records of rejected papers were found to be filed in alphabetical order; accepted papers, in chronological order. These two groups constituted the sampling frame, from which all manuscripts awaiting decision were excluded.

From each of the alphabetically ordered "rejected" folders a random sample of cases was drawn. A mean of 4.7 cases was taken from each folder. If a folder contained few or no cases, extra records were drawn from the subsequent folder. From the chronologically ordered records of accepted papers, a systematic sample was drawn. The selection interval was made small enough to allow for over-sampling of accepted papers, since during the past several years only about 13 percent of manuscripts submitted were eventually published. The final useable sample consisted of the records of 213 manuscripts, 42 percent of which were eventually published or slated for publication. In addition, information on 345 referees was gleaned from these records; this constitutes our second source of data.

Through these documents it was possible to estimate the length of the stages outlined in the previous section. Direct measures are available for the first two stages, and for the third and fourth stages when combined. The operational definitions are as follows:

Phase 1 Service Time. Time elapsed between date of receipt of manuscript to date of assignment to two referees.

Phase 2 Service Time. Time elapsed between date of assignment and the date on which the evaluation of the last referee is received.

Phase 3 Service Time. Time elapsed between date of receipt of last evaluation and date on which the board's final decision is communicated to the author.

The documents furnish no direct information on the interval between receipt of the final outside evaluation and the date of the board's decision. However, we shall find that a most convincing assumption can be made about the average length of this phase. An additional dependent variable was measured, namely, the reading time for referees who examined and evaluated the manuscripts.

The following independent variables were coded with a view to accounting for within-phase variations in manuscript delays:

Author and referee characteristics
  1. Cartter ranking (1966) of departments with which author and referees are affiliated;[1]
  2. Faculty status of author and referees;[2]
  3. Professional age of author and referees (years elapsed since receipt of last degree).[3]
Manuscript characteristics
  1. Length of paper;
  2. Content of paper;
  3. Referee's recommendation with respect to publication;
  4. Eventual disposition: paper accepted or rejected by editorial board.

It was also possible to determine the month and year manuscripts were received from and sent to authors and referees; the number of referees who read or refused to read each manuscript; the length of referees' comments to authors; and whether or not apologies for delay were made to an author.

In addition to these quantitative data, the author, by virtue of his former position as associate editor, was able to study the editorial process first-hand. The vantage point of the participant observer allows him to describe many important features of the organization which would not be visible to an outside observer.

Some Qualifications

Before the results of this inquiry are detailed, it would be desirable to enumerate at least some of the more basic limits to their generalization. The first is that the journal we are studying is a social science publication; as such there is relatively little sensitivity to the question of priority of discovery, an issue which is so important in the physical sciences (Merton 1957 [1973]) and their publications (Reif 1961). Partly for this reason, physical scientists typically wait less time for editors' evaluation of their work than do social scientists. Secondly, the institutional setting of the present editorial organization affects contributors' waiting time in a way that may not be precisely duplicated elsewhere. As noted, the editorial board of the *American Journal of Sociology* is staffed by faculty members selected from the Department of Sociology of the University of Chicago. During the periods covered in this research, editorial work was performed on the members' own time and not deducted from their committee assignments and other obligations to the department. The managing editor and full-time assistant were the only paid employees of the University of Chicago Press. Thus, the editorial work of faculty members was undertaken without material compensation of any kind and under a heavy burden of other duties. This was work to which only a moderate priority, at the very best, could be accorded.

It might also be pointed out that the *American Journal of Sociology* has been and is a very popular publication. There is no assumption among its editors that the speed with which it processes papers affects its ability to attract high quality and significant material. In this respect, the journal is less dependent on authors than authors are on the journal. Accordingly, improvements in operations are generally made as a matter of principle, if and when they are made at all, and not in response to extrinsic considerations, like competition with other journals —to which a second thought has never been given.

Method for the selection of referees is another nonuniversal characteristic which affects processing time. The range of papers which face this editorial board always exceeds the scope of its own collective expertise. As a result, editors are more often than not called upon to assign papers to readers in fields they know very little about. (Unlike some boards, this one does not maintain a list of competent readers in the various subdisciplines.) The readers selected (sometimes from the contributor's own references) therefore tend to be the most visible people in their fields—precisely those whose time is also in demand by other journals, and invested in many other important activities as well. Needless to say, this tendency should not be exaggerated. Indeed, the journal's annually printed list of referees makes their variation in renown and achievement public knowledge. But one can admit this without denying the possible effects of different referee selection processes. Any circumscription of the pool of potentially effective referees must have its effects on the reading time phase of the manuscript queue, as well as its relation to the length of the other phases we shall investigate.

Another important respect in which this journal may differ from others is in its editorial philosophy. While this outlook has never been formalized, it nevertheless tends to be subject to periodic discussion, which is typically structured in terms of two polar alternatives. We shall call the first alternative the "informational theory" of journal editing; the second we shall call the "educational theory." The informational theory holds the *American Journal of Sociology* to be an organ of the sociological profession whose sole function is to publish the best of the research submitted to it. By contrast, the educational theory conceives of the journal not only as a medium of public information but also as an informal conduit for the exchange of ideas between specialized authorities and hundreds of less seasoned scholars doing research within their sphere of competence. It is in this latter sense that a journal may perform an educational as well as a purely informational function. Now, during the period of time covered by our investigation, the *American Journal of Sociology* leaned decisively toward the educational pole of this continuum. This is not to say that all rejected contributors received detailed editorial critiques of their papers; it is to say that many did—more, perhaps, on the average, than did contributors to other journals. This practice has, as we shall see, a very direct bearing on the length of time papers are delayed in the final phase of the processing system (after their fate with respect to publication has already been sealed).

Another characteristic of this journal, closely related to editorial philosophy, is the tendency to work along with the author of a potentially good paper and to require additional revisions before accepting papers which seem to be already publishable. These tendencies are reflected in the fact that only one published paper in three is accepted without being returned for mandatory revision. And many if not most of the papers which are recorded as being accepted outright are actually accorded acceptances contingent on specific revisions; others are returned with specific suggestions as to how they might be improved. Thus, the post-decision waiting time of accepted as well as rejected manuscripts was extended by the journal's pronounced advisory tendencies.

The above are some of the factors which should be kept in mind as we turn to the extent and pattern of delay in the *American Journal of Sociology* manuscript queue.

Results

The data presented below allow us to estimate the relative contributions of editorial and referee delays to the total waiting time of manuscripts and their authors. This breakdown is made for the separate years 1969–72. Because of their small number, data for the years 1966–68 are combined.

The data consist of the 176 papers that were sent to at least one outside referee. This represents 82.6 percent of the total sample of 213. Eight, or 3.8 percent, of the manuscripts were returned to their authors without review because of the inappropriateness of their content. The remaining 29 (13.6 percent) were returned after an editorial reading confirmed initial suspicions regarding their suitability.

The analysis we are about to report was originally performed separately for papers which were eventually accepted by the journal and for those eventually rejected. In no instance could we find significant differences (or patterns of differences) in the queuing times of these two sets of manuscripts. While this outcome might be expected for phases 1 and 2, an advantage for accepted papers was suspected in phase 3, which contains the post-disposition queue. The reason for the assumption of faster processing for accepted papers in this phase is the simple necessity of preparing them for publication. That they are in fact not accorded priority may be explained in at least two ways.

The need for priority may be negated by the very sizable backlog of papers already slated for publication. (As with other organizations [Thompson 1967: 20], the journal "warehouses" its output in order to maintain constancy in its service process.) We have no direct data on waiting time in this particular "inventory queue," but we do know that during the last year studied it had consistently been twelve months or more. Secondly, the almost universal necessity for revision may cause the managing editor to actually devote more time drafting correspondence to authors of accepted papers, for whom the extensiveness and clarity of recommendations is most important. This tendency could offset any priorities that might be accorded to publishable material. At any rate, the absence of observable differences in the speed with which accepted and rejected papers are processed justifies our decision to combine and analyze them as a single unit.

We turn first to queuing time distributions in phase 1.

The row totals in table 6 show that 63, or 35 percent, of the manuscripts are processed out of phase 1 (assigned to referees) in one week or less; the remaining 65 percent are queued up longer. The mean for this distribution is 2.2 weeks. The table also shows that phase 1 queuing time was longest in the period up to and including 1968, when only 13 percent of the papers were processed within one week and the mean queuing time was 3.2 weeks. Processing times for all subsequent years are comparable, varying little around a two week mean.

The distributions for phase 2 queuing time are displayed in

TABLE 6.   Percentage Distribution of Manuscript Queuing Time by Year: Phase 1

	Year					
Weeks	−1968	1969	1970	1971	1972	Total
1	13(3)	29(10)	46(13)	37(19)	45(18)	35(63)
2	22(5)	47(16)	39(11)	33(17)	15(6)	31(55)
3	31(7)	9(3)	7(2)	18(9)	25(10)	18(31)
4	17(4)	9(3)	4(1)	10(5)	10(4)	10(17)
5+	17(4)	6(2)	4(1)	2(1)	5(2)	6(10)
Total	100(23)	100(34)	100(28)	100(51)	100(40)	100(176)
Mean[a]	3.2	2.2	1.8	2.0	2.1	2.2

Note: Number of cases given in parentheses.

[a]Means were computed from ungrouped data in this and subsequent tables.

table 7. The row totals for this table show that 37 percent of the manuscripts assigned are returned by *both* referees within one month after their assignment; 74 percent are returned within two months, and 85 percent within three. Fifteen percent of the manuscripts spend more than three months in phase 2. The mean for this total distribution is exactly eight weeks.

Year-specific means and distributions up to and including 1971 vary about their aggregate mean of 7.4 weeks and do not significantly differ from one another; however, the 1972 phase 2 mean of 10.2 weeks is significantly higher $(P < .10)$ than the combined mean for all preceding years. Separate data show that this increase is not caused by changes in the number of referees reading or refusing to read papers. Most importantly, there is no difference in respect to actual referee reading times. For the years up to and including 1971 the mean reading time is 4.5 weeks, which is almost identical to the figure for 1972. This datum suggests that the 1972 increase for phase 2 results from more frequent administrative, not reader, delays. Assigned papers are apparently waiting longer to be mailed out, for they are not waiting longer to be disposed of, once returned.

When the journal receives its final outside evaluation, the manuscript is scheduled for disposition at the next meeting of the editorial board. Although we have no independent measure of this "disposition time" interval, one may assume it to be almost identical with phase 1 processing time. This is simply because reviewed papers are placed in the same editorial board work queue as new manuscripts. It is true that the editor or an associate editor will act as third referee whenever there is significant disagreement in the evaluations of the first two.

TABLE 7.   Percentage Distribution of Manuscript Queuing Time by Year: Phase 2

Weeks	Year					Total
	−1968	1969	1970	1971	1972	
1–4	35(8)	35(12)	46(13)	41(20)	27(11)	37(64)
5–8	44(10)	41(14)	25(7)	33(16)	45(18)	37(65)
9–12	4(1)	9(3)	11(3)	14(7)	12(5)	11(19)
13–16		6(2)	14(4)	6(3)	8(3)	7(12)
17 +	17(4)	9(3)	4(1)	6(3)	8(3)	8(14)
Total	100(23)	100(34)	100(28)	100(49)	100(40)	100(174)
Mean	8.5	7.0	7.1	7.2	10.2	8.0

However, this procedure causes a delay in the disposition of only a small percentage of papers. (Furthermore, that delay is usually no more than the two weeks between board meetings.) Accordingly, if we take phase 1 as a surrogate for disposition time and subtract that quantity from the phase 3 measurement (which, as we may recall, includes disposition time) we may arrive at a rough estimate of how long it actually takes for the journal to communicate the board's decision to an author.

Let us begin, however, by tracing the gross phase 3 measurement over time. The bottom row of table 8 shows that, up to and including 1970, phase 3 queuing time varied from 4.2 to 4.4 weeks. Then, in 1971, this figure rose to a significantly higher level of nine weeks (P <.05) and by 1972 it had tripled by rising to twelve weeks.

The distributions for total phase 3 queuing time are shown in the body of table 8. Before 1971, over 70 percent of all manuscripts were processed within four weeks; after 1971 this figure dropped to below 40 percent. Looking toward the other end of the distribution, we find less than 5 percent of the pre-1971 manuscripts queued up for more than twelve weeks;

TABLE 8.   Percentage Distribution of Manuscript Queuing Time by Year: Phase 3

Weeks	Year					Total
	−1968	1969	1970	1971	1972	
1–4	79(18)	70(24)	71(20)	39(20)	30(12)	53(94)
5–8	13(3)	18(6)	18(5)	23(12)	15(6)	18(32)
9–12	4(1)	9(3)	7(2)	16(8)	17(7)	12(21)
13–16		3(1)	4(1)	6(3)	20(8)	8(13)
17+	4(1)			16(8)	17(7)	9(16)
Total	100(23)	100(34)	100(28)	100(51)	99(40)	100(176)
Estimated mean disposition time[a]						
	3.2	2.2	1.8	2.0	2.1	2.2
Estimated mean post-disposition time[b]						
	1.0	2.1	2.6	7.0	10.0	5.2
Total phase 3 mean						
	4.2	4.3	4.4	9.0	12.1	7.4

[a]These estimates are taken directly from the last row of table 6.

[b]This estimate is obtained by subtracting estimated mean disposition time from the total phase 3 mean.

the corresponding figure for 1971 and 1972 (combined) is almost 30 percent.

If our assumption about the approximate comparability of phase 1 and "disposition time" is correct, then most of a manuscript's time in 1971–72 is spent waiting to be returned to its author. While little variation is observed over time in the surrogate "disposition queue" mean of 2.2 weeks, estimated "post-disposition" queuing time has increased from an average of two weeks in the years preceding 1971 to seven and ten weeks in 1971 and 1972 respectively.

The recent prolongation of the phase 3 post-disposition queue has had a pronounced effect on and indeed accounts for most of the recent increase in total manuscript queuing time, whose distributions are presented below. The mean queuing times listed at the bottom of this table show an increase from an average of fourteen weeks in the pre-1971 period to 18.2 and 24.4 weeks in 1971 and 1972 respectively. The distributions show that in the years before 1971, at least 48 percent of all manuscripts were processed within a three-month period; this figure dropped to 37 percent in 1971 and to 28 percent in 1972.

We may summarize the findings from another standpoint. Mean processing times of 2.2, 8.0, and 7.4 weeks have been found for phases 1, 2, and 3 respectively. As we examine the year-specific means, however, we discover that total waiting time for manuscripts has increased dramatically in recent years, rising from 13.3 weeks in 1970 through 18.2 weeks in 1971 to 24.4 weeks in 1972. This represents an increment of almost three months. The source of this sharp rise is not to be found in phase

TABLE 9.   Percentage Distribution of Manuscript Queuing Time by Year: Total for All Phases

Weeks	Year					Total
	−1968	1969	1970	1971	1972	
5–12	48(11)	56(19)	54(15)	37(19)	28(11)	43(75)
13–20	26(6)	32(11)	39(11)	33(17)	20(8)	30(53)
21–28	17(4)	9(3)	7(2)	12(6)	32(13)	16(28)
29–36	9(2)	3(1)		10(5)	15(6)	8(14)
37+				8(4)	5(2)	3(6)
Total	100(23)	100(34)	100(28)	100(51)	100(40)	100(176)
Mean	15.9	13.5	13.3	18.2	24.4	17.6

1, where waiting time has been fairly constant since 1968. The phase 2 delay has also remained relatively stable, with the exception of a three week increase from 1971 to 1972. Without doubt, the most pronounced increase occurs in phase 3 where a previous four week mean processing time rose to nine weeks in 1971 and to twelve weeks in 1972. Phase 3 queuing time has almost tripled since the pre-1971 period.

The differential contributions of the three processing phases to total manuscript queuing time is to be found in table 10, where phase-specific means are expressed as percentages of the total mean wait. The table shows that the phase 1 percentage contribution has dropped from 20 percent in the earliest time period to 9 percent in the latest. Despite the recent absolute increase in phase 2 service time, its percentage contribution to the total has dropped from 53 to 42 percent. The phase 3 contribution, on the other hand, has almost doubled, rising from 27 percent up to 1968 (inclusive) to 49 percent in 1972. The major source of manuscript delay has thus shifted from phase 2 to phase 3. There is no doubt that the increase in post-disposition delay is responsible for this.

Such variation cannot be explained in terms of changes in the journal's personnel. During the years covered by this investigation the journal was under the same editor, and since late 1968 the managing editor has been the same. There has been turnover in the group of associate editors, but their number has not changed.

The most dramatic transformation is in the scope and magnitude of journal activities, some aspects and measures of which are furnished in table 11. The general tendency is one of

TABLE 10.   Phase-Specific Contributions to Total Manuscript Queuing Time by Year

| Phase | Year | | | | | Total |
	−1968	1969	1970	1971	1972	
1	20	16	14	11	9	13
2	53	52	53	40	42	45
3	27	32	33	49	49	42
Total	100	100	100	100	100	100

Note: Phase-specific mean processing time as a percentage of total processing time.

TABLE 11.   Volume of Activity by Year

Activity	Year			
	1969	1970	1971	1972
Manuscripts Received[a]	356	385	440	528
Articles & Notes Published	60	56	72	68
Book Reviews Published[a]	108	120	142	147
Total Pages	781	1001	1271	1400
Hours per Week[b]	55	65	65	70

[a]Figures derived from fiscal year (July to June) records by allocating 50 percent of the fiscal quantities to each calendar year.

[b]Managing editor and assistant.

increase. Specifically, the number of manuscripts received has risen at an increasing rate from 356 in 1969 to 528 in 1972. And not only were more articles and notes published in 1972 (68) than in 1969 (60); the 1972 contributions were also longer, on the average.[4] During this same period of time the number of book reviews rose from 108 to 147. These trends are reflected in the increase in total pages printed from 1969 (781 pages) to 1972 (1400 pages).

The last row of table 11 shows that in 1972 there were fifteen more clerical hours per week available to the journal than there were in 1969. These figures represent the amount of time the managing editor and clerical assistant put in per week, assuming a constant estimate of forty hours for the former. A separate computation demonstrates that the two most important sources of work, manuscripts received and number of papers printed, have shown increases, per clerical hour, over the past four years. However, these trends would appear in even bolder relief if they were based on total manhours available to the journal, for the editor's and associate editors' hours have probably remained constant over time.

Whatever its ambiguities, table 11 shows that the workload of the journal has risen over the past few years. One may still ask whether this increase has been sharp enough to warrant a 300 percent rise in observed phase 3 manuscript delay. (The rise in estimated post-disposition delay is even sharper.) And this question in turn raises the problem of whether the upswing in waiting time might have something to do with subtle changes in the work habits of the journal's personnel. We cannot rule out that possibility, but there are certainly other avenues to explore before resorting to it as an explanation.

We must first note that processing of low priority work tends to be very sensitive to fluctuations in total workload. The top priority tasks of the journal are easy to define: they include the "production" activities which precede each bimonthly publica-tion—for example, reading and correcting galley proofs, ar-ranging and ordering "makeup," reading and checking page and reproduction proofs, and so forth—as well as selection of publishable manuscripts. These jobs are vitally important because the journal cannot be published until they are com-pleted. It therefore comes as no surprise that as the number of printed pages expands and the amount of editorial and produc-tion work increases, a smaller proportion of available time is devoted to manuscript processing in the post-disposition part of phase 3. Indeed, it is conceivable that post-disposition work may be squeezed out almost entirely, for the lower the priority of a job, the greater the rate of increase in delay per unit increase in total workload. Put in more general terms, the effect on waiting time of workload-personnel ratios differs in accor-dance with the priority rating of tasks.

Is this to say that a contributor's waiting time is to be explained by some variant of a simple supply-demand model? The answer to this question is yes, insofar as the ratio of work to workers is associated with backlogs, and, no, insofar as this model fails to attend to the secondary processes to which the backlog itself gives rise. In this latter respect, an interview with the managing editor proved to be most useful. The point was made that until the recent upsurge in manuscripts received, the journal was diligent in returning papers to their authors as soon as possible—an observation that coincides with our data, which demonstrate sharp increases during the past two years in both manuscripts received and post-disposition delays. As the pile of papers waiting to be returned grows bigger, however, it receives increasingly less, not more, attention. "I look over and see this mountain of work," explains the managing editor. "So I decide to chip away at it by sending off five or six papers. The mountain looks a little smaller. I then turn around and find that fifteen more papers have been added to it. The hell with it, I figure. The mountain will never go away."

The remarkable thing about this attitude is that it parallels the point of view taken by servers in other kinds of organizations. For example, at the medical emergency department connected with the University of Chicago we were told that doctors work as fast as they can during slack periods, the object being to keep the queue as small as possible, or to empty the waiting room altogether. But as the peak hours approach and the queue becomes massive, the doctors give up and moderate the pace of their activity. They cease to care that patients are waiting precisely because there are so many of them. In the face of urgent demand they exude an air of casualness and detachment.[5] Such is the case in the present organization. The longer the queue, the less attention it gets. It is as if an operant principle governed the behavior of servers, in that effort expended on behalf of small queues produces a more visible impact than an identical amount of effort directed toward larger ones. If the effect of work (perceived accomplishment, so to speak) may be considered a kind of "reinforcement," then the tendency to devote less time to longer queues would be consistent with the operant formulation, which states that behavior is a function of its consequences (Skinner 1953).

But secondary processes arise from and act back upon this initial principle. As service time becomes longer, an especially clear and extended account of the editorial decision becomes mandatory—as a sort of compensation for the delay. After all, a paper held for five to six months or more cannot simply be returned to its author with a formal rejection notice. In this sense, justificatory information is exchanged for waiting time. In addition, careful apologies (whose expression is highly related to total processing time [$r = .44$]) must be formulated and this further augments average time spent per manuscript, once a decision is finally made to process it for return. Such a tendency not only lengthens waiting time but also creates new kinds of work, for the longer manuscripts are held, the more inquiries about them come in by phone (which interrupts ongoing tasks), not to mention the more numerous mailed inquiries, which are organized into a separate queue awaiting the attention of an already overwhelmed clerical worker. What we seem to be faced with, then, is a vicious cycle: once it has grown beyond a certain point, the very existence of a queue activates processes which further lengthen it.

The factors which prolong the time it takes to get a paper back to its author do not impede the flow of manuscripts in earlier stages of the editorial process. Despite a very sharp increase in total workload there has been no increase in the number of papers waiting to be processed out of phase 1. And while it seems to be taking longer to actually get papers assigned to referees into the mail, they are disposed of swiftly once returned. No backlog of manuscripts slated for adjudication by the board has developed. Thus, congestion is limited almost exclusively to the post-disposition phase. How is this tendency maintained?

Simple effort furnishes one reason for the pattern: it takes much more time for the managing editor to prepare a manuscript for return to its author than to simply set it before the editorial board. In the first case, a statement must be composed; in the latter, a filed manuscript and evaluation are only to be located and placed in a pile for others to work on. On the other hand, the board assigns and disposes of manuscripts in fairly large numbers; while little time may be devoted to locating a single paper, to bring together a large batch of manuscripts takes much longer. Yet this work is always done on time.

The reason for this consistency is to be found in the very terms by which it is described: manuscripts processed according to a formal routine have a short waiting time; papers not subject to routine administration wait much longer. This means that work assigned to staff with a definite deadline tends to be performed on time; when no deadline exists there is likely to be procrastination.

The above statement sounds very much like Parkinson's Law, whose partial applicability to the present case we have no reason to doubt. Unfortunately, total reliance on such a neat principle requires that we confine ourselves to isolated parts of the editorial system and ignore the operation of the system as a whole. The meeting of deadlines is after all not accomplished without cost, without diverting time from other potential uses, some referents for which are to be found in the post-disposition phase. Efficiency and short waiting time in one part of a service system are therefore brought about at the cost of ineffectiveness and long waiting times in other parts. One may phrase this differently: delays in one sphere of operations are promoted *in order to* maintain efficiency in other spheres. This assertion, which suggests that an organization may actually encourage ineffectiveness in one aspect of its operations, helps make sense out of a fact that would be otherwise unintelligible, namely, that post-disposition administration is the only part of editorial operations not subject to a deadline.

The foregoing argument does not fully explain why the post-disposition phase is chosen to absorb the delays and inefficiencies that could in principle be more evenly distributed throughout all phases. Why this particularly one-sided allocation of delay? The immediate reason seems plain enough: selection of publishable papers from those submitted is the principal function of journal editing, and the present allocation maximizes the efficiency with which this function is performed. By contrast, the delay which occurs after the selection process is completed does not undermine the achievement of this basic organizational goal. But this only means that the efficiency of the system is ultimately maintained at the expense of its clients. Accordingly, their contributions may be processed according to the principle of "Hurry up and wait."

Within-Phase Variations

Up to now we have investigated the duration of manuscript delay in the different phases of the service process. We have also seen how these queuing times have changed over the past several years. We presently turn from the question of absolute delay to the order in which manuscripts are processed.

Every organization which in some way treats people (or things related to them) makes use of a "queue discipline," that is to say, a set of decision rules which govern the order in which service is to be rendered. In many service systems the basic priority principle is the rule of "first come, first served." At the same time there is a recognition of contingencies which entitle a person to faster service. These may be referred to as "preemptive priorities,"[6] in that they allow some clients to take the place of earlier arrivals.

Two kinds of preemptive priorities, formal and informal, are to be distinguished. Formal exceptions to the principle of order of arrival give expression to an explicit organizational policy which requires that they be made; informal priorities are imposed without official legitimation. Informal priorities manifest themselves for a number of reasons. They may reflect interests and prejudices, or they may help negate the dysfunctional consequences of an excessively rigid adherence to the principle of "first come, first served." On the other hand, if interests, prejudices, or dysfunctional consequences are absent —or at least contained—then informal priorities may not be systematically imposed at all.

In the present investigation we sought to identify the queue discipline which governed the processing of manuscripts. Actually, no explicit policy regarding priority has ever existed for the *American Journal of Sociology*. In practice, however, papers seem to be processed in accordance with the order of their arrival. This is made possible by the technique of piling, whereby manuscripts are stacked face-down on top of one another; by simply turning over the pile and working from the top, the speed with which a paper is processed will directly correspond to the order of its arrival in the pile. However, this technique may be circumvented by placing an incoming paper on the bottom rather than the top of a stacked queue. To do so would be to accord a preemptive priority.

Of the theoretically infinite number of grounds for preemptive priority, we chose to focus on measures relating to authors' professional status and institutional affiliation. The importance of these variables inheres in the question of whether the distribution of power and prestige in a profession is maintained (or undermined) by patterned differentials in temporal access to editorial service. If better-known authors from the more prestigious institutions are in fact accorded favorable priorities, then the queuing time of their manuscripts should reflect their superior academic status.

Table 12 displays the correlations between the Cartter ranking of the author's department, his professorial rank, his professional age, and the queuing time for his manuscript in each of the phases of the editorial processing system. Correlations with total processing time are also included. These coefficients are not only consistent with a true value of zero in phase 2, where the author's identity is not known, but in phase 3, too, where it is. The correlation coefficients listed under total service time

TABLE 12.   Zero-Order Correlations between Authors' Affiliation, Faculty
Rank, Professional Age, and Manuscript Queuing Time by Phase

Variable	Phase			Total Service Time
	1	2	3	
Authors' Departmental Affiliation (Cartter Rank)	.108	.120	.076	-.002
	(76)	(75)	(76)	(76)
Authors' Faculty Rank	-.063	.006	.031	.105
	(121)	(119)	(120)	(121)
Authors' Professional Age	.173[a]	-.153	.160	.043
	(98)	(96)	(97)	(98)

Note: Number of cases involved in computation given in parentheses.

[a]Correlation significant beyond .10 level.

also conform to a null hypothesis of zero relationship. Under
phase 1, the correlation between professional age and service
time (.173) is significant beyond the .10 level. However, there is
good reason to assume that a relationship of this magnitude
could have been generated by chance. For if each of a set of
twelve correlation coefficients is compared with a .10 significance criterion, .10 x 12 or 1.2 of these coefficients may be
expected to exceed the .10 level even if all are generated by a
random process. Because the one significant correlation falls
within this interval we may assume that it does not necessarily
indicate a true relationship.

Although these findings relate to only that portion of the total
sample for which background data were available, they are
consistent with the assumption that academic status plays no
role in the queue discipline of the *American Journal of Sociology*. With a view to evaluating the possibility that status factors
are activated only when editors are inundated with manuscripts
and when the time available per manuscript becomes ex-
ceedingly scarce, we repeated the above procedure for the years
up to 1970 and for 1971–72, when the journal's activities
increased so sharply. A separate analysis showed no discernable
differences in these two sets of data.

As far as the manuscript itself is concerned, only one characteristic seemed to be important. The correlations between the

number of manuscript pages and processing time turned out to be .115, .173, .186, and .276 in phases 1, 2, 3 and for total service time, respectively. The latter three coefficients are significant beyond the .10 level.[7] Thus, the longer the paper, the longer it takes for it to be processed out of phases 2 and 3. There were no differences associated with content of manuscript (the eleven content categories included theory, methodology, and nine substantive areas).

Taken together, these findings warrant the conclusion that, for manuscripts of a given length, order of arrival routinely governs order of service. This is emphatically not to say that preemptive priorities are never accorded on the basis of the author's characteristics; rather, it means that they are not accorded in a systematic way. Thus, anyone who has spent even the least amount of time in the editorial office knows that when a request for priority is made, it will usually be granted if deemed legitimate. For example, the author whose promotion may hinge on the journal's decision may receive immediate attention. Or a phone call made at the appropriate time may yield information on the disposition of a paper that is resting in the post-disposition queue. However, priorities such as these are bestowed as personal favors and are not assigned on a routine basis.

We also sought to determine whether the characteristics of the 289 referees who read and returned papers in any way affected the speed with which they did so. The initial assumption was that referees associated with the more prestigious departments, or of highest rank within their own, might take longer to evaluate manuscripts because of greater demands on their time. A possible counter-assumption is that referees are productive in their own right and dependent upon journals as outlets for their work; for this reason the most visible (i.e., productive) reviewers may be the most indebted to the journal and so provide the fastest service. The outcome of our analysis suggests that these opposing tendencies may cancel each other out. The correlations between reading time and Cartter ranking of referees' department, professorial rank and professional age are .00, –.02, and –.06, respectively.[8] Each of these coefficients is well within the range of a null hypothesis of zero correlation. However, reading time was found to be correlated with number of manuscript pages (.193) and length of remarks to author (.488); it was unassociated with content and recommendation as to worthiness for publication.[9]

Summary

What can we now say to the irritated contributor who is still waiting for word on a paper he submitted several months ago? How can we explain this delay to him? The one thing to be said with certainty is that he should not take it personally. The delay has nothing to do with his academic affiliation or status. It has nothing to do with the content or quality of the manuscript itself. Nor does it relate to the academic status of the readers to whom the manuscript is sent. He can be sure that, when its length is taken into account, his paper is being treated on a "first come, first served" basis. But if delays are not associated with the preferences and characteristics of the people who take part in administering a service system, then they must derive from properties specific to the system itself. By tracing out this line of inquiry we have no difficulty in discovering where the problem lies. It has to do with differential priorities not within but among queues.

The phase 1 queue is a high priority queue: most manuscripts are assigned to readers without delay, given the frequency of board meetings. And to schedule these meetings closer together would only reduce the author's waiting time by a few days. The expectant contributor might blame the readers for delaying his manuscript, and they do account for part of the problem, but not so great a part as was perhaps first imagined. The average referee will actually take a little over a month to read and evaluate a paper. Phase 2 service time may be substantially increased, however, when a paper is originally assigned to a person who cannot read it, or when a person fails to receive or return a paper. Then new reviewers may be assigned and much time is lost. But even when these and other contingencies, such as the mail queue, are taken into account, phase 2 seems to be no more important a source of delay than the time it takes to administer the paper after it is handled by referees. In fact, for persons who have recently submitted a manuscript to the *American Journal of Sociology*, the greater portion of waiting time is spent after, not before, the fate of their paper has been officially decided.

It is important for the contributor to know that when he submits a manuscript to this journal he competes not only for its limited pages but also for the scarce time of its personnel. He should also know that in view of the indispensable editorial and production work that precedes the publication of each issue of the journal, the job of processing his paper through a final administrative phase will receive relatively low priority; that function will be performed only when the earlier work, for which there is a deadline, has been completed. Furthermore, we tried to show that as the amount of high priority work increases, the time ordinarily devoted to processing papers back to their authors can be reduced to almost zero.[10] The phase 3 post-disposition backlog built up by this tendency is only intensified by another to which the backlog itself gives rise: because identical service produces a proportionately weaker effect on the size of large queues than on the size of smaller ones, the server seems to experience less reward in dealing with the former, and so reduces its priority further. This tendency, as we showed, is not a peculiar one; it obtains in different kinds of organizations. A general psychological principle is thus super-added to the objective relations of supply and demand in the determination of phase 3 post-disposition queuing time. But, whatever their source, the outcome of these tendencies is to subserve the journal's goal of rapid identification of publishable manuscripts. If a deadline for returning papers to authors were set and delays more equitably distributed among earlier pro-cessing phases, the efficiency with which this objective is met would be seriously undermined. Put differently, tolerance of the long post-disposition queue protects the core functions of the journal by "buffering" or absorbing the effect of fluctuations in manuscript input (see Thompson 1967: 19–23). The empirical tendency to devote least effort to the most congested part of the queuing system is thus grounded in the interests of that system, and, ultimately, in its capacity to ignore the interests of clients.

What has been said may be cast in more formal terms. Any service system must decide what kind of processing equilibrium it wishes to maintain: (1) stability of the service process or

(2) stability of the queue. Constancy in either one of these respects implies variation in the other. Thus, if a service or administrative technique exhibits stability in the face of growing demand, the size of the queue will fluctuate in accordance with this demand; or if queue size is designated as the constant, then the service process must be transient in order to offset variations in demand. Our investigation has shown that a different equilibrium can be maintained for each phase of a service system. Short queues are continually maintained in phase 1 and, to a somewhat lesser extent, in phase 2, by allocating most of the journal's increased manhours to the administrative activities associated with them; in the post-disposition phase, however, service has remained constant (and may have even decreased), while the queue has been allowed to lengthen. The consequence of this arrangement is to maximize the effectiveness with which the journal pursues its primary goals of selecting and publishing the most worthy manuscripts, and to minimize the costs of doing so.

The most general significance of what we have said is that queues (provided they are strategically placed) are *not* to be construed as system problems; rather, they represent solutions to these problems. This is because congestion in a "peripheral" segment of a social organization subserves the efficiency of its core functions. This principle becomes most important in an organization which lacks control over the magnitude and timing of its input. By slowing down a peripheral function, the system can respond rapidly and adequately to demands on its essential operations.

In concluding, however, we do not wish to give the impression that a substantial reduction of post-disposition service time would interfere with the efficiency of other operations if the factors which remained constant during the period of time studied were caused to vary in an appropriate direction. A de-emphasis of the "educational" responsibilities of the journal, or any other change that would reduce the time devoted to preparing a paper for return would reduce author delay. A general reorganization of the editorial system could perform the same function. In addition to these measures, the introduction of direct appeals to referees (coupled with the assurance that a speedy evaluation will not encourage the editors to inundate them with more papers) could cut a week or so off the average reading time. (For evidence, see Rodman 1970.) In short, a disturbance of any combination of the constants we have depended upon could reduce (or, for that matter, increase) authors' waiting time without invalidating the conclusions drawn while they were in effect.[11]

2 Priorities in Client Processing

4   Queue Discipline

Delay and congestion are relevant to the analysis of public order as well as formal organization, to which we have so far devoted most of our attention. Two frameworks are currently employed in the study of public behavior. The first is concerned with the structure and process of orderly human intercourse (see, for example, Goffman 1963, 1971); the second, known as "collective behavior," deals with the conditions which transform peaceful and predictable relationships into mobs, panics, and riots. The analysis of queuing and waiting is situated at the intersection of these two standpoints. It converges with the first as it seeks to discover the norms which regulate the sequences in which people routinely satisfy their needs; with the second, because it explores the ways these arrangements can fall apart.

Queuing and waiting relate to public order in two senses. On the one hand, the queuing process is structured in its own right; on the other, a broader system of human traffic depends on its stability. If that commerce (whether it be vehicular or pedestrian) is to proceed smoothly, those engaged in it must be relied upon to wait periodically. The well-regulated traffic system must not only coordinate different lines of action but must also adjust these activities to organized lines of inaction.

However, there is little manifest advantage to being inactive in a queue: that much can be said about waiting—at least from the standpoint of the person doing it. Waiting is disadvantageous economically because it entails the renunciation of more profitable kinds of activity; psychologically, because it is often boring and may imply a disregard for the value of a person's time and social worth. These considerations give rise to a classic problem: if delay tends to undermine the rational interests of individuals, how are irrational conflicts among them managed

91

and orderly queues (and, thereby, public order) maintained? The objective of this chapter is to provide at least tentative answers to this question.

Definitions

Two basic terms, "server" and "waiter," relate to all queuing phenomena. By server, we refer to a person who is able to provide others with some social or economic benefit. The waiter is simply one who anticipates being accommodated. (The terms "waiter" and "client," in contrast to popular usage, can be employed interchangeably.)

Of course, the server-waiter distinction is not entirely satisfactory. There are circumstances, such as two friends arranging to meet somewhere at a particular time, in which the server-waiter division is only a latent one; servership or waitership becomes a contingency of order of arrival. This is the case in all scheduled encounters. Even in formal relationships, the server may sometimes have to wait (and so expend "idle time") until the tardy client appears for his appointment. However, there exists a class of engagements in which incumbency in server and waiter roles is more clearly predefined. These can be observed wherever people gather for unscheduled service: at department stores, supermarkets, restaurants, theaters, post offices, banks, highway toll-booths, public transportation terminals, and so on. These diverse units are organized around the same basic structure, which consists of one or more "service facilities" and one or more "waiting channels." Within this framework waiting can be defined most precisely: it is the time that elapses between the moment a client enters the waiting channel and the moment he is served.[1]

Waiting and Scarcity

A queue whose volume is constant over time is said to be in a "steady state," which is approximated to the extent that organizations offset fluctuations in client demand by addition or subtraction of servers and/or by accelerating or decelerating service time. When these steps are not taken, the state of the queue becomes "transient" and vacillates in size from one period of time to the next. Given temporal fluctuation in the number of clients entering a service system, then, a steady state of the queue presupposes a transient state of the service facility, while constancy in service occasions variations in queue volume. From this standpoint, waiting is understood to be occasioned by scarcity of access to goods and services.

Queue Discipline

Were only one person at a time to wait, the appearance of order in the face of scarcity would be a psychological rather than a sociological problem. However, the prerequisite of allocation and its decision rules emerges when more than one person awaits the same unscheduled service, for "competitive allocation cannot operate without institutionalization of norms defining the limits of legitimate action, particularly in this case with regard to legitimacy of means of attaining the goal" (Parsons 1951: 197).

Presumably, the problem of allocation has to do not only with *how much* different persons are to be given from a finite supply of goods and services but also with the *priority* in which their needs are to be satisfied. Although both perspectives address each aspect of the issue, it may be said that stratification theory focuses on the issue of *quantity* while the theory of queuing emphasizes the problem of *priority*. Queuing theory is in this sense an extension of stratification theory. However, it is insufficient to merely say that solution of the "allocation problem" requires institutionalization of a normative distribution principle. More importantly, disciplined allocation is the single alternative to expropriation by coercion. But this point requires that we proceed much further, for to say that waiting is an orderly accommodation to scarcity is only to describe one function of the queue, not the moral norms that make it orderly.

The Service Priority Principle

The rule that perhaps most commonly informs the phenomenon of queue discipline among unscheduled arrivals is "order of arrival," popularly referred to as "first come, first served." Because it stands as a reference point for variations, this principle (in western societies, at least) constitutes the normative basis for most[2] forms of queuing.

Anchored in the relationship between priority of investment (time spent in a queue) and priority of reward (order of service), the rule of "first come, first served" may be subsumed under those broader principles which demand the equilibration of investments and rewards (Homans 1961: 75).[3] In Mann's (1969: 346) words, "if a person is willing to invest large amounts of time and suffering in an activity, people who believe there should be an appropriate fit between effort and reward will respect his right to priority."

It follows that resentment and anger generated by violations of equitable allocations of place arise not because victims' *interests* have been subverted but, rather, because the *rule* by which they govern themselves is contravened. Cooley (1964: 281–82) made this point most explicitly when he wrote:

> Suppose one has to stand in line at the post office, with a crowd of other people, waiting to get his mail. There are delay and discomfort to be borne; but these he will take with composure because he sees that they are part of the necessary conditions of the situation, which all must submit to alike. Suppose, however, that while patiently waiting his turn he notices someone else, who has come in later, edging into the line ahead of him. Then he will certainly be angry. *The delay threatened is only a matter of a few seconds; but here is a question of justice, a case for indignation, a chance for anger to come forth.* (Emphasis added)

The rule of "first come, first served" thus points to a relative temporal cost as opposed to mere position as the legitimator of priority of service. It is respect for this outlay which makes queues as orderly as they are.

Of course, we do not presume to account for order in queuing by the mere invocation of a principle that demands it. That would be altogether redundant. More importantly, it would leave unexplained conformity to that principle, which, though it be "fair" or "distributively just," is second nature to no one. In fact, the subordination of personal needs to an impersonal allocation principle must with difficulty and in the face of great resistance be inculcated in infancy, by systematic deferral of gratification, and in childhood, by compelling the impatient to "take turns" in organized games. The young, then, do not wait of their own accord.

Furthermore, the adult's commitment to the rule of "first come, first served" does not presuppose renunciation of infan-

tile and childish inclinations. Indeed, just the opposite conclusion is warranted. Were there no persistent and deeply-installed
propensity to violate it, the rule itself (and commitment to it)
would be altogether superfluous. Accordingly, far from inferring
from maturity an attraction to queue discipline, we rather
assume a tendency not to defer to the needs of others, at least
while one's own needs press for immediate satisfaction. The
very persistence of the queuing rule is thus itself proof of a
persisting and general inclination toward what it prohibits.

Accordingly, when we take the standpoint of individuals
arriving at the end of a long line, we sense imperatives which
have nothing immediately to do with distributive rules. It
would not be unreasonable to assume, in fact, that many are
deterred from trying to expropriate the place of others ahead of
them solely by anticipation of the vocal or physical resistance
that that attempt would provoke. What keeps the typical client
in his place, then, is not devotion to principle but reluctance to
"create a scene"[4] by making himself conspicuous—along, perhaps, with a premonition that he might not be attended to at all
were he to cause a disturbance.

This inference may help explain the limited frequency with
which clients blatantly edge into a line ahead of others, why
queues tend to be jumped at their most ambiguously ordered
parts when they *are* violated. Thus, in supermarkets, a customer
may edge in ahead of those who leave a considerable space
between themselves and the person ahead of them, making
ready to claim he was not aware of what he had done, if
challenged. Or shoppers with more than eight items may use the
eight-item limit express counter, claiming an innocent miscount
if called upon to account for themselves. Similarly, in cafeterias
those who fail to close ranks may be accused of procrastinating
over their selection and deemed worthy of bypass. In other
settings, queues are more often jumped by (willing or unwilling)
proxy. At racetracks, for example, a violator may without
breaking into the line itself approach a forward position and ask
its incumbent to place bets for him, taking advantage of the
victim's interest in not causing an incident by brusquely turning
down a request for an intrinsically simple favor. Elsewhere,
people may collude with accommodating friends in line to
obtain what they need.

The theme running through these instances is that when queue discipline is ignored, it is usually ignored inconspicuously. It is as if conventional inhibitions against the creation of troublesome and embarrassing scenes governed the conduct of the offender as well as the victim. Queue discipline is in fact traceable to restraint on the part of both. On the one hand, when vital interests are not at stake, the victim will not always overtly object to an inconspicuous usurpation of his place, for that kind of intrusion does not put him in the awkward position of having to dramatize his unwillingness to humiliatingly submit to gross public abuse. This being so, he may consider as not worthwhile the spectacle of open rebuff, for the considerable social cost of an incident would exceed the negligible benefit of saving a few moments of waiting time. On the other hand, if a victim is willing to overlook a violation that does not undermine his dignity, so is the potential offender deterred by the possibility that it might. And even the actual offender, by the very deviousness of his method, exhibits deference toward and in so doing protects the honor of his victim.

All of this is to say that orderly queues do not necessarily presuppose consensual devotion to the rule of "first come, first served" but may give more direct expression to mutual restraint and accommodation between the more and less impatient. Accordingly, the chaotic dissolution of the queue can be forestalled not only by the default of deviance but also by its contingent toleration.

If, as we have said, a well-ordered queuing process can be maintained in the face of sporadic violation of the queue discipline, it follows that total conformity to the rule of "first come, first served" (and full renunciation of the impulses which oppose it) would render that order altogether nonproblematic. But this inference flows from our not having said enough. It results from an approach that, while focusing upon the tensions of self-denial effected by disciplined allocation, ignores the strains occasioned by contradictions within the allocation rule itself.

Preemptive Priorities

The coordination of order of arrival and order of service does not in itself solve the problem of equitable priority allocation.

This is because the costs of waiting and rewards of service differ in magnitude as well as priority, and, what is worse, may vary in a random rather than a systematic fashion. Such incongruence is further exacerbated by *need*, which has classically stood as an alternative to costs and investments as a legitimate allocation principle.[5] All of which means that while service in order of arrival is generally thought to be "fair," not all arrangements that satisfy this standard accord prior service to first arrivals. Everywhere we find rules which permit those with presumably high priority needs or demanding lesser service to preempt the place of and so be processed before those who enter a queue earlier. These rules constitute "preemptive priorities," or authorized exceptions to the criterion of order of arrival. The conditions which give rise to preemptive priorities should be explored more thoroughly.

Precisely because it is equitable in terms of temporal costs, the principle of order of arrival inevitably gives rise to situations which are patently inequitable from the standpoint of need. In a bank or in some other commercial establishment, for example, clients are frequently distressed when, after moving quickly toward a cashier, they find that the person immediately ahead of them requires complicated and extensive service the duration of which delays them in a measure disproportionate to their inferior priority. The situation appears irrational both to them and to others behind them, and may even embarrass the one who causes the delay. This shared sense of absurdity would be felt even more acutely if accident victims rushed to an emergency room had to wait their turn before being treated, or if a client who merely needed a form to be signed had to wait behind all previously scheduled clients demanding extensive service, or if a shopper with a few purchases had to wait behind others who would take up far more of the server's time. Preemptive priorities are therefore useful because they allow urgency and extensiveness of need to temper strict adherence to priority of arrival as a criterion for the allocation of service. They allow the emergency case to be seen immediately, the client requiring simple authorization to go ahead of others and get it, the shopper with a few items to go to an express counter, and so forth.[6]

In general, services are granted first to those who need them most, regardless of the time it takes to administer them. However, superior priorities tend also to be granted to those whose needs can be met with little effort and do not significantly interfere with the administration of more lengthy or complicated services. This "decision rule" helps to insure at least a minimal level of correspondence between the costs a client incurs by having to wait for a service and the costs a server incurs in granting them, while at the same time according to urgent needs an appropriately favorable priority. The consequence of this system is to minimize the size of the queue and so reduce the expected waiting time of the typical arrival.

Queue Disorganization

It bears emphasizing that preemptive priorities do not necessarily contradict the standard of fair exchange; on the contrary, they are actually demanded by it when strict application of the criterion of "first come, first served" gives rise to irrational modes of allocation. Accordingly, within each preemptive category the rule of "first come, first served" typically prevails. In this way, fairness is maintained within and between queues.

But preemptive priorities are not always institutionalized; some are in fact "expropriated" rather than legitimately allocated. Giving expression to no consensually recognized rule, these illegitimate preemptions indicate breakdown in queue discipline. The potential for such disorder is present in all queues. We may once again state that the rule of "first come, first served" would be unnecessary in the absence of a general inclination of the latest arrivals to wish immediate service. While its execution is typically renounced for the sake of public order, that wish remains, finding individual expression in an often acute sense of impatience. Assuming all of this to be so, there must be an ambivalent attitude toward the value of queue discipline, which accounts for a general willingness to disregard it. However, willingness to transgress the ground rules of waiting does not in itself suffice to account for their actual violation. For this, there must be opportunity as well.

Channelization and Visibility of Place

Illegitimate opportunity is a property of service systems; this is why the rule of "first come, first served" is situationally variable in its application. Specifically, queue discipline is always tightest in those settings which provide the best ecological supports for it. These include queuing channels created by cords, such as are found in theaters, and painted lines or railings in other establishments. However, the most radical queue-prop is to be found in some American military induction centers, where perfect rows of outlines of human feet are painted on the floor leading to examination stations; therein candidates are advised to sequentially position themselves as they move from one station to the next.

When a waiting area has not been physically channelized, however, it is more difficult to dramatize the cost to which the reward of prior service is supposed to correspond. Failure to provide means for the dramatization or registration of place gives rise to an anomic condition, for it precludes the application or enforcement of any allocation rule whatever. What appears then is a non-rule: "service in random order." Here is an opportunity for the latest arrival to be satisfied first, and a risk for the earliest arrival, who may be served last. Queue disorganization finds precise definition in this arrangement, wherein order of service is unpredictable, given knowledge of order of arrival.

Chaotic service systems present themselves in many contexts, ranging from crowded department store sales counters on bargain days to subways at rush hour. Regardless of context, however, the anomic form is invariant: being unable to tell exactly where to line up, or to ascertain who preceded whom in terms of order of arrival, each considers himself entitled to priority. The incontestable rationality of this *individual* assumption evolves often into the drama of *collective* irrationality: pushing, shoving, bickering, and a general disorder that delays everyone.

Order and Disorder in Non-Channelized Settings

Though channelization is an important feature of orderly waiting areas, it is common knowledge that not all orderly queues are channelized. In fact, service in random order is a theoretical model that is frequently approximated but hardly ever realized empirically. Several factors account for this. For one, absence of ecological supports may be the occasion for administrative ones when disorderly queues undermine the interests of servers as well as clients. Thus, an organization may impose and enforce an allocation criterion by granting service in accordance with an arrival list kept by a server, by mechanical number dispensers whereby customers learn of their place, and so on.[7]

In these latter kinds of arrangements there is a distinct technical advantage over lined queues. While the line admits of a measure of inherent stability in that its constituents are placed in "face-to-back relations" with, and are therefore socially isolated from, one another,[8] the line also represents a visible opportunity structure for queue violators, all the more inviting because it demonstrates in a rather precise way where the violation is likely to be most successful and do the most good. When there is no distinct line of people, however, there is really nothing for the would-be violator to edge into, unless it be the list upon which he may by some not unheard-of means impose himself. Still, in doing so, he creates no disturbance within the waiting channel itself.

Potentially random systems may be patterned in other ways. The absence of ecological supports may, under some conditions, be the occasion for very complex ground rules which make for priority ranking in terms of order of arrival, but with the help of neither physical ordering, which a lined queue provides, nor administrative control over service sequence. For example, if a few or several people await a bus at a particular corner, or a train on a certain part of a platform, each can take into account the order of another's arrival as they make ready to board, taking care to step aside for the sake of those who arrived before them or even to grant preemptive priority in accord with honorific[9] criteria. The same arrangement helps preserve a semblance of order in many other settings.

However, when more than several persons are waiting, it is most difficult to assess one's own order of arrival in reference to everyone else in the waiting area; but it is possible to take account of arrival time in reference to those who are positioned in close proximity to oneself. This makes a measure of queue discipline possible—but *only* a measure. Brown (1965: 716–17) describes such a condition in a resort hotel:

> By five minutes of six there were more people in the lobby than could be seated in the dining room. Promenading was no

longer possible and each guest took a stationary position dictated by an implicit social contract. There was no line but there was an order and it was a just order. Without standing one behind another the guests could calculate their beeline distances from the door and the guests who had been longer in the lobby were nearer the door whereas those who had come down more recently were farther from the door. When the door should be opened, if each guest would walk, not run, to the door the probability that he would be admitted would be proportionate to the length of his wait. Exactly as if the guests had formed a line. . . . An outsider would have thought the guests were haphazardly scattered about the lobby.

The implicit order threatened to become explicit whenever a recent arrival undertook to move a bit closer. People in apparently casual postures proved surprisingly unwilling to step aside. Openings one had seen just ahead closed as one approached. Eyes hardened, chins squared and you stayed where you were.

Exactly on the hour the maitre d'hotel moved to the dining-room door and slowly drew it open. He turned to greet the first guest and just missed being trampled to death.

The above is an instance of a "partially ordered queue" whose members are not accommodated in strict order of arrival; priority is rather *associated* with their arrival time. The partially ordered queue may be situated between the fully ordered queue that is strictly administered on the basis of "first come, first served" and the totally disordered queue whose constituents are served in random order. More precisely, these three types of queue discipline occupy points on an axis at whose respective poles priority of service (given preemptive priorities) is uniquely determined by and randomly related to order of arrival. This variation raises two questions: (1) What arrangements are necessary for service to be apportioned in accord with order of arrival? and (2) What conditions must obtain to effect break-down in totally or partially ordered queues? If we extend the scope of our discussion just a bit further, both questions may be more pointedly addressed.

Queue Panic

As has been shown, the stability of a line is affected by physical, mechanical, and normative "channelization" of the waiting area. It has not been made clear, however, that channelization is only the medium of client discipline and can in no way be construed to account for it. Accordingly, we are no further along in answering the question originally posed; we can only phrase that question in a different way: Given a particular medium for structuring service priority, what principles maintain or subvert the order of the queuing process?

One thing seems certain. Queue discipline is never problematic when the service for whose sake the queue forms remains altogether inaccessible. To confirm this we need only recall Brown's observation of the partially ordered dining room queue. That formation collapsed only when the dining room doors were opened at the appointed hour, before which access was out of the question. Nor is queue discipline in jeopardy when the service to which it provides access promises to be available to all who seek it. Note, for instance, how Brown prefaces his observations with the initial statement that "there were more people in the lobby than could be seated in the dining room." Were the opposite condition to prevail, and seats be presumed to outnumber occupants, the partially ordered queue's transformation into a disorderly one would be, at most, unnecessary, and, at least, unexplainable. Queue discipline seems to be problematic when the acquisition of *service* is problematic, and when the need for that service is felt to be imperative and cannot as cheaply or easily be met by a substitute. This is to say that breakdown of queue discipline requires transformation of the service system's exchange structure.

That last point demands elaboration. We need first to recognize that equilibration of supply and demand is the most conspicuous economic function of waiting. Given a limited supply of servers, anticipated waiting time may cause persons to renege from a queue after having joined it, or to balk or refuse to join it in the first place. These occurrences suppress demand. Given a certain level of demand (queue size), on the other hand, more servers may be provided or existing servers may work harder to handle more clients per time unit. This increases access and, with it, demand. Waiting time is in this light functionally similar to the phenomenon of price, which is to say that it is part of the price exacted for a service. The parallel also follows the extremes of price. Too much waiting time renders the server inaccessible; no waiting time makes him a "free" commodity. In most cases, however, service is accessible but scarce; accordingly, the person desiring it must wait. But this is no more than an "economic" principle; the sociological corollary is that that person must remain disciplined as he waits— otherwise, the service system is plunged into chaos, rendering further transaction impossible.

However, the satisfaction of sociological imperatives is conditioned in part by economic contingencies. Thus, queue discipline will break down when (1) the discrepancy between supply and demand cannot be relieved by reneging or balking; (2) the need for service is objectively or perceptively imperative (i.e., inelastic); (3) it is perceived that service must be granted within a very short time if it is to be effective; and (4) agents who would normally enforce queue discipline are consequently caught off-guard, present in too few numbers, or ill equipped to cope with the resulting disorder.

Exit Disorder

One may imagine a large number of people simultaneously seeking rapid departure from a public place following the normal termination of some event. There may be a bit of pushing and shoving, and even an incident here and there, but the evacuation process itself will be characterized by order, if not speed. However, let a condition be introduced that brings with it collective urgency and the need for immediate egress; then the queuing structure will change.

Many of the more tragic hotel, club, and theater fires (at least those reported in the collective behavior literature) bring large numbers of people face to face with such an extraordinary condition; they accordingly admit of a common pattern: following the onset of a conflagration, quasi-queues or loosely organized lines (sometimes supervised by offical or heroic self-appointed agents) may begin to make toward service (exiting) points; in other instances a more disciplined line is formed. But at some point panic ensues as one or more persons break for the exits. Simultaneously, the queue itself dissolves as client demand overwhelms service capacity. Because the size of an exit limits its simultaneous use to at most two or three people, the many more seeking to pass through it may form a literal cork; bodies piled on top of one another close off the exit, and what was formerly a service area is transformed into a deadly waiting channel. Eddie Foy (1957: 96–97) provides a concrete example in his description of the famous Iroquois Theater fire:

> As I ran around back of the rear drop, I could hear the murmur of excitement growing in the audience. Somebody had of course yelled "Fire!" . . . The crowd was beginning to surge toward the doors and already showing signs of a stampede. Those on the lower floor were not so badly frightened as those in the more dangerous balcony and gallery. Up there they were falling into panic.
>
> It was said that some of the exit doors leading from the upper tiers onto the fire-escapes on the alley between Randolph and Lake Street were either rusted or frozen. They were finally burst open, but precious moments had been lost—moments which meant death for many behind those doors. The fire-escape ladders could not accommodate the crowd, and many fell or jumped to death on the pavement below. Some were not killed only because they landed on the cushion of bodies of those who had gone before.
>
> But it was inside the house that the greatest loss of life occurred, especially on the stairways leading down from the second balcony. Here most of the dead were trampled or smothered, though many jumped or fell over the balustrade to the floor of the foyer. In places on the stairways, particularly where a turn caused a jam, bodies were piled seven or eight deep. Firemen and police confronted a sickening task in disentangling them. An occasional living person was found in the heaps, but most of these were terribly injured. The heel prints on the dead faces mutely testified to the cruel fact that human animals stricken by terror are as mad and ruthless as stampeding cattle. Many bodies had the clothes torn from them, and some had the flesh trodden from their bones.

Breakdown in queue discipline may derive from an altogether rational individual decision and act when the ongoing service rate fails to guarantee or prohibits satisfaction of imperative needs. In these circumstances, those at the end of the queue have everything to gain and nothing to lose by ignoring the "first come, first served" rule. This helps account for Turner and

Killian's (1957: 95) observation that, in panic-stricken queues, "It is *pressure from the rear* that causes those at the front to be smothered, crushed or trampled." Irrationality in the breaking of queue discipline is thus situated at the *collective* level alone. On the other hand, when orderly exit guarantees survival for all, collective and individual irrationality coincide. Note, however, that once queue discipline breaks down and the desire for exit overwhelms exit capacity, the principle "every man for himself" is for every man the most rational one. [10]

Incidentally, the possibility and consequences of exit disorder inform such evacuation exercises as fire drills. While most common in public schools, these rituals perform the latent function of socializing children for orderly waiting for exit from establishments in which they will find themselves as adults. The maneuvers are therefore to be understood as general training in queue discipline. They are deemed instrumental to preventing the condition that invokes the rule of "every man for himself."

Entrance Disorder

When demand is massive, queue discipline becomes a prerequisite not only for leaving an establishment but also for entering it. Discipline in the latter respect is especially important because the maintenance of order after persons have entered a system is often very much dependent on whether or not it has been possible to control their entry. Failure to do so subjects that system to inundation. Thus, at the Valentino funeral:

> The doors were actually opened a little after two o'clock. With a shout the crowd rushed forward, bowling the police aside and threatening for an instant to wreck the inside of Campbell's place.
> When the crowd started going through the gold room the Campbell attendants found they had another problem on their hands. Nearly half of those in line tried to reach for some souvenir of the occasion, and it was clear that some would succeed and probably ruin the room. So the line was stopped at the lower doors, and the coffin moved to a smaller room one flight up.   (*The New York Times*, August 25, 1926: 1)

Inundation is a consequence of breakdown in discipline

among queues offering access to an establishment; as such, it is to be understood in terms of the same contingencies which occasion exit disorder. In both cases, urgent, inelastic needs overcome both the tendency to renege and balk and the constraints imposed by queue-disciplining agents. However, while *exit* disorder draws our attention to the urgency of need for departure as a precondition for collective panic, *entrance* disorder, because it admits of the options of reneging and balking, highlights the default of preparedness in enforcement modes. Of this, the Valentino affair furnishes an especially useful illustration:

> During the morning, before it had been definitely an-
> nounced that Valentino's body would lie in state and the
> public be admitted, a crowd of five or six hundred gathered,
> giving the police some trouble. In the early afternoon, the
> crowd swelled to about 10,000 and kept growing. There were
> then a dozen foot policemen and two mounted men on the
> scene. . . .
> At first there had been little or no attempt to get the crowd
> into line at any distance from the doors. Hence the constant
> disorder and the breaking of windows. Slowly, lines were
> formed, half a block long. At the far end of the line police
> stood and tried to hold the mass back. Slowly, time and again,
> the mass pushed forward, a foot at a time, even shoving the
> horses along the sidewalk, so great was the pressure from
> behind. When the throng got too close to the doors and the
> single file was shortened, the police charged, driving their
> horses into the crowd, breaking it up, pushing it back to the
> corners.
> So bad was a break that came at a little after six o'clock
> that it seemed likely the crowd would run down the police
> and flock into the main entrance in a body. Reinforcements
> were sent for, and the place was closed for an hour. . . .
> Along the line, too, people from across the street were
> constantly trying to break in. Seven mounted men and fifteen
> on foot tried to hold the crowd back, but failed often. The
> tactics of the afternoon had to be resorted to.   (*The New
> York Times*, August 25, 1926: 3)

The above is but a dramatic instance of the prerequisite of boundary maintenance in the distribution of service. It is an extraordinary case because it concerns a queue of macroscopic proportions. However, we have seen that the vicissitudes in the social order of this kind of queue are subject to the same conditions which bear on those with which by reason of routine participation we are all familiar. The hundreds of people who seek to view a great figure or event and the few who struggle with one another for a seat on a bus all find themselves subject to the same principles. Because these principles help make intelligible the discord as well as the order of queues, they represent points of analytic convergence for the riotous instances subsumed under "collective behavior" and the normal forms brought together under the rubric of "public behavior." The continuity between these polar conceptions is embodied in the determinants of queue discipline.

Conclusions

The objective of this chapter was to identify some of the conventional and emergent norms, structures, and processes that make for order and disorder in crowded waiting areas. We have tried to show that queue discipline is promoted by consensual recognition of an impersonal principle governing priority (the rule of "first come, first served") and, as well, by a preemptive priority principle that specifies exceptions to this rule—which helps to resolve its occasional inconsistency with the broader principles (distributive justice, fair exchange, etc.) under which it is subsumed. As was also shown, the normative regulation and order of queues is affected by the power of enforcement agents, opportunity for reneging and balking, ecological supports, and urgency and elasticity of demand. Queue discipline thus gives expression to conditions operating at the cultural, organizational, situational, and personality levels. Implied here, moreover, is a hierarchical organization of levels, with the cultural norm providing the code (normal and preemptive priorities) whose translation into action is facilitated or inhibited by the lower level (organizational, situational, and need) contingencies.

The analysis itself has focused on what occurs in service systems within, not among, different cultural settings. We therefore assumed a level of ambivalent commitment to the rule of "first come, first served," then tried to specify some of the conditions which affect its application. This limitation is of course self-imposed and does not imply a denial of variation in organized commitment to the rule itself. Indeed, that rule appears to be an expression of a more general value structure historically associated with (though by no means confined to) Western society. "To us," claims Hall (1959: 157–58), "it is regarded as a democratic virtue for people to be served without reference to the rank they hold in their occupational group. The rich and poor alike are accorded equal opportunity to buy and be waited upon in order of arrival.... As a general rule [therefore], whenever services are involved we feel that people should queue up.... This reflects the basic equalitarianism of our culture." However, there are distinct variations within the Western world. Respect for order of arrival perhaps achieves its most pronounced expression among the English (see, for example, Lee 1966: 115),[11] and seems to be least conspicuous among some Eastern European groups (Hall 1959: 158; 1966: 128, 162). But these are very broad and speculative generalizations, not the kind of detailed and validated knowledge we need to extend the significance of our observations. The cultural anchorage and conditioning of the norm of "first come, first served," its preemptive priorities, physical organization of service systems, and clients' attitudes toward the constraints they impose, stand therefore as conspicuous gaps in the theory of queue discipline.

The above assessment holds true in a very important and practical sense. After all, the sociological theory of queuing seeks not only to make waiting intelligible but predictable as well. On its face, though, it would seem that no objective could be more readily achieved independently of cultural variations. For, if waiting is governed by supply of and demand for service, then it must be derivable from distribution of arrival and service times alone. However, without some adherence to a queue discipline, service priority would no longer follow from order of arrival—or contingencies which preempt the latter—and the system's input and service time would then not yield accurate estimates of waiting time for individual clients. In many cases, of course, assumptions about queue discipline may be easily accepted. This is especially true where the constituents of a service system are things rather than human beings. (An inventory of goods waiting to be processed out of a warehouse may be taken as an example.) But when the "elements" of a queue are aware of themselves and their place in the system, assumptions about queue discipline need to be advanced more cautiously. For queue discipline is then confounded by the most complex system of priorities which are often not only vague and resistant to explicit formulation but which also vary, in ways sometime obvious but often subtle, from one cultural and sub-cultural context to the next. By identifying the more basic properties of queuing structures, then, we have only cut through part of this ambiguity. In so doing, however, we have at least made intelligible some of the more basic conditions of public order.

5   Formal and Informal Priorities in an Emergency Medical Treatment System

Allocation is one invariant point of reference for the analysis of social systems in general (Parsons 1951a: 114–36; 1951b: 197–208) and health care delivery systems in particular (Perlman 1969). It is a function which has not only to do with *how much* different clients are to be apportioned from a finite supply of medical goods and services but also with the priority in which their needs are to be satisfied. This distinction admits in turn of two questions: (1) how is priority (waiting time) distributed within medical service systems? and (2) among clients assigned a given relative priority, what accounts for the actual magnitude of their delay? A patient's absolute waiting time is related to the collective demand for the kind of medical care he seeks and the extent and organization of its supply; relative delay, however, is governed by a more or less complex set of allocation rules, otherwise known as a *queue discipline*.

Queue Discipline:
The Formal and Informal Models

Order of arrival is the normative basis for most forms of queuing in medical and other systems which render unscheduled service. Anchored in the relationship between priority of arrival (time spent in a queue) and priority of reward (order of service), the rule of "first come, first served" may be subsumed under the broader allocation principle of "distributive justice." However, not all arrangements which seem fair to us allow prior service to first arrivals. Everywhere we find rules which dictate that persons with special kinds of needs be processed before those who enter a queue earlier. These constitute *preemptive priorities*, or authorized exceptions to the principle of order of arrival.

Preemptive priorities are characteristic of the queue discipline that prevails in most emergency departments. A patient there will normally have to wait until earlier arrivals are treated only if their physical conditions are comparable to his own; if his ailment demands more urgent care, it is considered proper that he be assigned a superior priority and preempt their claims.

When the probability of circumventing the "normal rule" of "first come, first served" is a unique function of a client's physical state, the preemptive priority is said to be invoked by a "universalistic-achievement" criterion. Priority is thereby allocated impersonally and in accordance with a consensually validated "achievement" (illness or acute physical need). However, another basis for assigning priority to a patient's needs is his place in the social order. For, despite a formal commitment to "affectively neutral" and "universalistic" standards, emergency room practice is often conducted with much affect indeed, and sometimes reflects the "particularistic" notions of moral worth which prevail in the society-at-large (Roth 1972). Preemptive priorities may thus be anchored in the moral evaluation of a patient's social status, independently of his objective physical needs. Because the consideration of social worth in medical processing is strictly proscribed by professional and institutional standards, assignments of priority on such a basis can be made only on an unofficial or "informal" level.

That the strictly moral appraisal of a client affects the promptness and care with which treatment is administered is a pivotal fact in the sociology of medical organizations. (See, for example, Glaser and Strauss 1965; Sudnow 1967.) However, it is one thing to assert or demonstrate that a patient's assumed personal worthiness will affect the kind of care he receives; it is another matter to show such regard to be substantively important. At question is whether moral considerations even approach, let alone overshadow, the importance of medical indicators as determinants of patient processing and treatment. The purpose of the present investigation is to address this issue.

Race as a Preemptive Priority

The medical status of a patient may be indexed by a rating scale (to be described below) which indicates the acuteness of his physical complaint. As to measures of moral status, we shall confine ourselves to one characteristic that, in our society, is very often taken to be an indicator of personal worth, namely, skin color. Historically, the moral evaluation of the Negro has had great consequences for the allocation of goods and services of all kinds. This has been as true in respect of priority as of quantity. In other words, color has been a traditional element of queue discipline in American service systems.[1] These micro-organizations have in turn given expression to subcultural and institutional variations on the salience of race—at least in nonmedical settings. The old South was perhaps prototypical in this respect. There, blacks were always expected to relinquish their place in line to white persons who joined it later than they (Doyle 1937). Regardless of their urgency or the time it would take for them to be met, the needs of those deemed inferior were simply assigned lower priority than the needs of members of the more worthy caste. The realm of "train etiquette" may be taken as an example:

> If a number of persons of both races is awaiting the arrival of a car, the white persons will generally board the car first. . . . Two Negro women from Texarkana, Texas were fined ten dollars each for violating the rule in Columbia, South Carolina. . . . Generally, Negroes do not eat in the dining cars on the trains. Yet aboard some trains this has been remedied to the extent of permitting Negro passengers to enter the dining car after all white passengers have been served. (Doyle 1937: 148, 232–33; 150)

The importance of color was even maintained in the queue discipline of the most impersonal and rational organizations. Writes Doyle (1937: 153): "Commercial relations, generally conceded to be those least affected by the mores, have in the south not been entirely able . . . to free themselves from the incubus of taboo. In the stores white customers are all waited on, in general, before any Negro patron is served." In more or less subtle ways, this order of priorities maintains itself throughout many of our contemporary institutions, both North and South. Its recognition is perhaps best expressed in the slogan of those who are routinely subjected to it: "If you're white, all right. But if you're black, step back."

The specific purpose of this investigation is to determine the relative importance of race as a preemptive priority in the queue discipline of a contemporary northern metropolitan emergency medical treatment system.

Data Collection and Measurement

The materials on which this study is based were gathered in connection with the Chicago Survey on Emergency Medical Services. Part of the data and method of collection were described in chapter 2, "Emergency Department Structure and Waiting Time." The present investigation makes use of one additional source of information: namely, interviews conducted with all patients seeking treatment during a twenty-four hour period in seventy of eighty Cook County, Illinois, emergency departments.

The typical procedure for data collection was for the investigator to situate himself near the intake desk where a client could be interviewed as soon as he was admitted. If a person was taken directly to a treatment room, he would be interviewed later, or material would later be obtained from the intake clerk or supervising nurse. This procedure yielded 2,944 cases.

Our objectives require reasonably accurate estimates of a patient's waiting time, his physical and social status, and the amount of congestion in the emergency department he visits. These dimensions were measured with varying degrees of accuracy.

Waiting time is defined as the amount of time that passes between the moment a patient is formally admitted to the emergency service system by a nurse or registration clerk and the time he is seen by a doctor. This datum was directly recorded by the on-site interviewer. Delays following the initial contact with the physician (e.g., waiting for lab tests, X-rays, etc.) were not recorded.

A measurement of medical urgency was obtained by means of a Clinical Urgency Rating scale. The attending physician was instructed by the investigator to indicate the seriousness of a patient's condition by describing it along the following three-point continuum:

1. *Emergent.* Requires immediate attention. Delay is harmful to patient. Disorder is acute. Potentially threatens life or function.
2. *Urgent.* Requires medical attention within a few hours. Danger if not attended. Disorder is acute, but not necessarily severe.

3. *Nonurgent.* Does not require the resources of an emergency service. Disorder is minor, or nonacute in severity.

Information on medical urgency was available for 2,563 cases, or 87 percent, of the total sample.[2]

Because effects attributed to race may actually be related to social characteristics associated with it, five additional status dimensions were measured and employed as controls. These include age, sex, and marital status—all observed by the interviewer or reported by the respondent. Marital status is to be entered into the analysis as a dichotomy: never married (single) and ever married (married, separated, divorced, or widowed). In addition, crude estimates of socioeconomic status were made by the interviewer's determination of a patient's education (highest grade achieved) and whether or not he possessed medical insurance.

In order to obtain a direct measure of queue size at the time of a patient's entry into an emergency unit, it would have been necessary to ascertain the times of arrival and treatment for every patient at each of the seventy hospitals, with the number of untreated prior arrivals also recorded for all of the 2,944 patients in the sample. To get around this very costly procedure, we decided to use a surrogate variable. Our assumption was that if we controlled for the the time of day he enters the unit (during a busy or slack period) and the number of servers provided at this time, then the absolute volume of demand on the emergency room (on the day a patient makes his own demand) may be taken as an index of congestion. Assuming constancy in service and time of arrival, then, persons who enter a very "popular" emergency department are more likely to join a longer queue than those who visit a less popular facility.

Of all the measures taken, there is no doubt that the medical urgency index is most open to question. On the one hand, we cannot be certain there would be full agreement in the ratings of patients if two or more doctors were called upon to assign them. This means that the scale is probably less than fully reliable. On the other hand, there is probably variation within each of the three categories of urgency, which means that the scale is not perfectly valid. These weaknesses will suppress the observed associations between the urgency rating and other measures, including waiting time.[3] Whatever their level, however, we have no reason to assume that reliability and validity coefficients are not similar from one part of the sample to the next; measurement error and bias[4] will therefore not affect the propriety of our comparison of urgency effects among groups. But we must exercise a great deal of caution in comparing the effects of urgency and race, since the latter's association with waiting time is not attenuated by imperfect reliability and validity. Thus, if urgency and race effects are identical in the universe, we may expect to observe stronger race effects (although we cannot say what the expected observed difference, given no real difference, would be).

But there is another problem. What is most determinative of a patient's wait is not the treating physician's assessment of the acuteness of his disorder but rather the judgment of the nurse or intake worker. (The rating of the doctor is assigned after the waiting period is over.) It is also true, however, that acute disorders are highly visible and readily differentiate themselves from chronic and minor disorders. This being so, we may assume a rather strong association between the ratings assigned at intake and those assigned after treatment by the doctor. Indeed, we were advised by one of the interviewers that after observing a hundred cases or so, she could predict the doctor's urgency rating with very high accuracy.

Before proceeding, we need to make explicit a point that bears on the interpretation of results. In this investigation, we are addressing ourselves to a general sample of emergency departments, and to subgroups within that sample. For this reason, there are no grounds for drawing inferences with respect to individual emergency departments. One of the inadequacies of this study, then, is that, like all analyses of general samples, it can only demonstrate the general tendencies in the determination of a phenomenon and so cannot inform the policy of particular organizations. Put differently, our focus is upon *system* and *sub-system* as opposed to *unit* tendencies.

Results
Determinants of Waiting Time

The Beta coefficients in table 13 provide estimates of the relative, independent effects on waiting time of congestion, medical urgency, and race.

A fairly sharp ordering is obtained by this methodology. Waiting time is shown to be affected most by congestion, or the

TABLE 13.   Relationship between Emergency Department Volume, Medical Urgency, Race,
and Waiting Time

| | Coefficient | |
Variables[a]	Beta	B
Department volume[b]	.264	.296*
Medical urgency[c]	.117	5.700*
Race[d]	.052	3.160*
Mean waiting time (in minutes)	22.89	

[a]Partialed on each other as well as department staffing,
volume and service at time of arrival (two-hour intervals),
sex, age, marital status, education, and insurance.
[b]Department volume mean = 55.65
[c]Emergency=1; urgent=2; nonurgent=3; mean=2.29
[d]White=1; Black=2; mean=1.38
*P < .01

volume of demand on an emergency room with service volume
constant (.264). The acuteness of a patient's physical condition
(.117) is of significantly lesser importance.

If priority were granted solely on the basis of patients' order of
arrival and physical condition (an allocation consistent with the
formal model of queue discipline), then all of the explained
variance in waiting time would be associated with the above
variables; the inclusion of race would not significantly add to
this quantity and the regression coefficient associated with it
would be consistent with a true value of zero. It turns out,
however, that with all other social status measures (age, sex,
marital status, education, and insurance) constant, race is
related to waiting time well beyond the .01 level. This outcome
indicates the presence of an allocation principle that cannot be
accounted for by the formal model of assigning priorities.
Regardless of their medical or social characteristics, or the
amount of congestion in the emergency room they visit, waiting
time is longer for blacks than for whites.

We may examine the importance of these determinants in
terms of their impact on the actual magnitude of delay. To do
this, we turn from normalized (Beta) to standard (B) regression
coefficients.

The daily volumes in the seventy emergency departments
range from 2 to 136 patients. Multiplying both ends of this

distribution by B, we obtain an *expected range* of waiting time of about one to forty minutes. As to medical urgency, the B coefficient shows that the "urgent" patient (coded 2) will on the average wait 5.7 minutes longer than the "emergent" case (coded 1), holding the values of all other variables constant. The "nonurgent" patients (coded 3) will wait 2 x 5.7 or 11.4 minutes longer than the emergent. The B value associated with race (which is entered as a dichotomy) admits of a very straightforward interpretation. The cost in units of waiting time of being black is B itself (i.e., 3.16 minutes). While this figure is inconsistent with a hypothesized difference of zero, it is not a very sizeable one. The discriminatory practice to which it gives expression must in fact be almost imperceptible to those subjected to it.[5]

Congestion and the Assignment of Priorities

Notwithstanding the statistical significance of their effects, it must be pointed out that less than 9 percent of waiting time variance is accounted for by volume, urgency, and race acting together. Even if we allow for the substantial degree of randomness inherent in waiting time differences among individuals,[6] this outcome reflects a surprisingly low level of predictability. Three facts seem to relate to and inform the result. In a separate analysis, we found that for all seventy hospitals the median daily emergency room volume is only thirty-nine patients, or about 1.6 patients per hour. At the same time, the median number of servers is 3.6. This ratio finds expression in a *median waiting time* of only 17 minutes, an expected delay to which few patients anywhere would object. These figures are not consistent with the universal image, drawn in bold detail by both administrators and staff, of an emergency treatment system inundated by walk-in patients with minor and chronic complaints (Roth 1971). In relation to available staff, in fact, demand on the typical emergency room seems to be very light, even though much of it may indeed belong elsewhere. At any rate, when only 1.6 cases arrive hourly in a facility staffed by 3.6 workers, an allocation rule (which is only necessary when a desired resource is scarce) may not be invoked at all; that is to say, no matter who they are or what kind of treatment they need, all patients may be seen almost immediately. We may therefore assume that it is only when demand substantially exceeds supply that servers are required to formulate (and act in accordance with) a queue discipline.

All of this suggests that the significant effects we have observed may be traced to a subset of the most inundated hospitals. We explored this possibility by dividing emergency units into five groups, ranging from those with the lowest daily volume (with a mean of ten patients a day) through emergency rooms of intermediate volume—averaging thirty, fifty, and seventy daily arrivals—to emergency departments which accommodated an average of ninety-five patients a day. The larger, most frequently visited emergency rooms are characterized by the smallest staffs in proportion to number of patients and longer "treatment" times.[8] The latter relationship is apparently due to differential secondary queuing for diagnostic services. The significant department volume Beta (table 13) also suggests that, because there is a greater variety of them, the smooth organization of services is most problematic in the larger facilities. (For evidence, see chapter 2.) Thus, volume of demand indirectly creates substantial inefficiencies in patient processing.[9]

By assessing the effects of urgency and race on waiting time within each of the five emergency department groups, we may identify the way preemptive priorities adjust themselves to measured increments in client demand.

Before constructing table 14, we found that for patients visiting emergency departments accommodating a very considerable range of client demand—up to seventy-nine arrivals per day—race and urgency Betas fluctuated relatively little. Furthermore, the magnitudes of these coefficients were not substantial.[10] What this means is that, up to a certain point, there is no relationship between the measure of demand to which an emergency department is subject and its tendency to discriminate on any basis in the assignment of priorities; beyond that point, however, there is a change. When the daily number of arrivals in an emergency system reaches eighty and beyond, an exceptionally visible allocation system emerges. We therefore combined all emergency rooms with a daily volume of seventy-nine or below and compared this group with units

TABLE 14.   Relationship between Medical Urgency, Race, and Waiting Time by Emergency Department Volume

| Variables[a] | Emergency Department Volume | | | |
| | –79 Daily Visits (n = 2354) | | 80 + Daily Visits (n = 590) | |
	Beta	B	Beta	B
Medical urgency	.147	5.437*	.208	12.745*
Race	.058	3.216*	.250	20.554*
Mean waiting time	20.95		30.65	

[a]Partialed on each other as well as department staffing, volume and service at time of arrival (two-hour intervals), sex, age, marital status, education, and insurance.
*$P < .01$

treating eighty or more patients a day (table 14). We found the relationship between race and waiting time to be almost five times as strong in the busiest and most congested departments (.250) as in the smaller units (.058). The urgency Beta also turned out to be higher in the most popular departments (.208 as against .147).

These differences may also be stated in terms of B coefficients: in the least frequently visited facilities, the nonurgent patient waits an average of 2 x 5.44, or almost eleven, minutes longer than the emergent. In the most inundated units, however, the nonurgent wait 25.5 minutes longer—with all other factors held constant. Similarly, the average Negro in a noncongested emergency room will be delayed 3.22 minutes longer than his white counterpart; but in a crowded emergency room the black will wait over 20 minutes longer than the average white patient.

In brief, the results disclose that while minor ailments increased waiting time in both groups of emergency rooms, this effect becomes disproportionately strong among clients of the most inundated units. Similarly, while the typical black patient tends to be kept waiting longer than the white who is comparable to him in all other measured respects, it is the black in the inundated facility whose delay is especially pronounced. It is thus when a service is most scarce that the socially despised or the patients who make illegitimate demands are most likely to face extra long waiting times. This finding conforms to a complex model of priority allocation, for it means that waiting time is explained not only by the additive effects of inundation, legitimacy of demand, and social worth, but also by their interaction. An exceptionally high number of arrivals in an emergency department may therefore be said to alleviate constraints on the interdependence of clients' race, medical urgency, and waiting time. The remarkable fact is that when this happens *race alone seems to explain at least as much waiting time variance as medical urgency.* (We employ the phrase "seems to explain" for the sake of caution, taking into account the greater reliability of the race measurement.)

Urgency and the Assignment of Priorities

We may now examine the data from a different standpoint. If the relative effects of race and urgency are contingent upon the level of demand to which an emergency system is subject, then we may expect the urgency of a patient's physical status to condition the relative effects on his waiting time of his race and the amount of congestion in the system he visits. Table 15 provides support for this assumption.

These results demonstrate that all patients are affected by the demand for service in an emergency department. However, the results also show the volume Beta to be over four times as large among the least urgent cases (.406 as against .114 and .080

TABLE 15.   Relationship between Emergency Department Volume, Race, and Waiting Time by Medical Urgency

	Medical Urgency[b]					
	Emergent (n = 260)		Urgent (n = 1309)		Nonurgent (n = 994)	
Variables[a]	Beta	B	Beta	B	Beta	B
Department volume	.114	.096	.080	.091*	.406	.431*
Race	−.059	−2.637	.068	3.795*	.066	3.829*
Mean waiting time	11.49		19.73		25.38	

[a]Partialed on each other as well as department staffing, volume and service at time of arrival (two-hour intervals), sex, age, marital status, education, and insurance.

[b]Number of missing cases = 381.

*P < .01.

among the emergent and urgent respectively). This simply means that the speed with which the more severe cases are treated is less dependent upon the length of the queue they enter than those who appear with nonacute disorders. Put differently, a unit increment in the daily volume of an emergency room will lead to four times longer a wait among the nonurgent than among the emergent and urgent. On the other hand, the Betas (and B's) related to race do not vary as significantly from one urgency level to the next. However, an interactive relationship may be inferred from the absence of a significant race effect among emergent patients.

Client Problems, Organization Problems, and Racial Discrimination

What conclusions may be drawn from these data with respect to the function of race in the queue discipline of medical emergency services? One thing is certain. If a medical good or service is available in abundance, then discrimination along any lines is least likely to occur. This is probably because benefits allotted to one person will not, under this condition, subvert the interests of another. When the supply of service is short in relation to demand, however, the "zero-sum" contingency is activated, whereby benefits to the despised client generate costs for the more worthy. For this reason, perhaps, allocation is most likely to follow racial lines under conditions of scarcity. This argument is consistent with the oft-heard observation that when "things get tough," it is the blacks who suffer the most.

However, our account is an incomplete one, for it fails to recognize two important facts: (1) that the patient who brings to the inundated emergency room a minor or otherwise illegitimate complaint will wait longer than the acutely ill patient (see the appropriate Beta coefficient in table 14); and (2) that the effect of race on waiting time vanishes when a patient's physical condition is acute (see table 15). These observations raise the question of whether the disadvantage of the black patient in the congested facility is maintained *regardless* of his medical needs.

In order to answer this question we must introduce the contingencies of client demand and medical urgency simultaneously rather than separately. This is undertaken in table 16, in which the effect of race on waiting time is examined among

TABLE 16.   Relationship between Race and Waiting Time by Emergency
Department Volume and Medical Urgency

| | Medical Urgency[b] | | | |
| | -79 Daily Arrivals | | 80 + Daily Arrivals | |
Variable[a]	Emergent/Urgent (n = 1300)	Nonurgent (n = 801)	Emergent/Urgent (n = 269)	Nonurgent (n = 193)
Waiting time (minutes)				
Black patients	20.0	22.4	19.7	57.6
White patients	17.5	20.6	17.6	24.0
Total	18.3	21.4	18.0	40.0
Percentage black[c]	33.6	46.7	21.2	47.1

| | Coefficients | | | | | | | |
	Beta	B	Beta	B	Beta	B	Beta	B
Race	.047	2.536	.042	1.835	.036	2.081	.338	33.59*

[a]Race partialed on department staffing, volume and service at time of arrival (two-hour intervals), sex, age, marital status, education, and insurance.
[b]Number of missing cases = 381.
[c]These percentages are approximations; see note 12 of this chapter.
*P <.01

nonurgent and urgent/emergent patients (combined because of the low number of emergent cases) in both the least and most popular emergency units.

The results show that in the emergency departments with the fewest patients the effect of race is relatively negligible among both the least urgent (Beta = .042) and most urgent patients (Beta = .047). Moreover, we find as we look at the most inundated facilities that the race effect is no more pronounced among the most urgent cases (Beta = .036) than for any group of patients in the least congested units. Sharp discrimination along racial lines occurs only among nonurgent patients who make demands upon already congested service systems. In this group the race Beta takes on a value of .338, over seven times as great as the value in any other cell. The corresponding B coefficient tells us that the Negro patient will wait no less than 33.6 minutes—over half an hour—longer than a white who is comparable to him in all other measured respects. In the other three cells, the black-white differences average out to about two minutes.

It remains for us to inquire into the distributional meaning of these patterned differentials in access to medical care. There are in this respect two possibilities: in nonurgent cases, (1) waiting time for white patients may be "reasonable," while blacks are called upon to wait longer than they should; or (2) black patients might experience a "reasonable" delay, while whites wait less time than they should. At question, then, is whether the observed inequalities result from blacks waiting too long or from whites not waiting long enough. All that is needed to answer this question are the data in the first and second rows of table 16.

Mean waiting times for black and white patients were computed by inserting into the regression equation the mean values for all the variables introduced as controls. Expected delay was then calculated for whites (coded 1) and blacks (coded 2). The difference between the resulting means equals coefficient B.

Looking first to the black patients, we observe the level of department volume exerting no effects on waiting time among urgent cases (20.0 – 19.7 minutes) but adding 35.2 (57.6 – 22.4) minutes to the waiting period of the nonurgent. On the other hand, medical urgency decreases waiting time by 37.9 (57.6 – 19.7) and 2.4 (22.4 – 20.0) minutes in the most and least congested emergency departments, respectively. For white patients, however, department volume increases waiting time by zero (17.6 – 17.5) and 3.4 (24.0 – 20.6) minutes among the most and least urgent cases, while in the most and least crowded facilities urgency decreases delay by 6.4 (24.0 – 17.6) and 3.1 (20.6 – 17.5) minutes. Although the direction of the latter relationship conforms to that of the former, the two differ markedly in respect to the magnitude of the interaction effect. In other words, while the mean waiting time for nonurgent blacks in the inundated facilities is at least thirty-five minutes longer than the expected wait under any other set of conditions, the comparable range for whites is no more than three and a half minutes. This means that the white patient who brings a minor or chronic ailment to the busy emergency room will not have to wait much longer than anyone else, while his black counterpart will face a much longer delay.

If there is inequity among these two sets of data, it must surely be in the first. It is after all perfectly fair for a non–bona fide emergency patient to wait a great deal longer than one who presents a legitimate demand for service; it is, on the other hand, quite unfair for a patient with a nonurgent condition to be treated almost as quickly, for this could only result in a delay for the more deserving. Accordingly, the data in table 16 suggest that racial discrimination in the processing of nonurgent patients in congested systems stems less from unreasonable delays for blacks than from whites not being kept waiting long enough.

Summary. When the demand on an emergency facility is limited, waiting time will be relatively brief and there will be minimum discrimination on the basis of either legitimacy of a request for treatment or the moral worthiness of a patient. Thus, table 16 shows a mean waiting time of 18.3 minutes for urgent cases in noncongested facilities, as compared to 21.4 minutes for the nonurgent—a difference of only three minutes. Corresponding race Betas of .047 and .042 are almost identical. Even in the inundated emergency rooms, waiting time and racial discrimination will be minimized when a patient presents a bona fide complaint. The mean waiting period (18 minutes) and race Beta (.036) are actually somewhat less pronounced here than in the cells referred to above. But when a patient brings a minor or chronic complaint into a congested system the mean waiting time rises dramatically to 40 minutes. However, this increase is mainly due to the longer waiting times imposed upon nonurgent black patients, who, in congested systems, wait about 38 minutes longer than the more urgent blacks; among whites, the comparable delay is no more than six and a half minutes longer. It must be stressed, however, that only 9 percent of the blacks bring minor ailments to inundated emergency rooms; the vast majority (91 percent) are subject to relatively negligible discrimination.

Discussion and Conclusions

A queue discipline, as we may recapitulate, is a set of transformation rules (explicit and implicit, formal and informal) which enable service systems to infer from the characteristics of patients the priority category to which they belong. However, we have seen that the amount of information contained in these characteristics, taken separately, is too small to completely specify the empirical priorities; rather, the details of the ordering are generated by the characteristics in interaction with one another. More precisely, in assigning priorities servers take into account order of arrival, urgency, and race, both separately and in combinations. The salience of any one priority criterion is thus contingent upon the value of another. In this sense, the additive rule of queue discipline is "over-demanding"; deviations from it constitute an adaptation to input contingencies whose variety is too broad to be subsumed under a simple model. Therefore, queue discipline may not be understood as an invariant allocational mode but, rather, as a strategy by which organizations accommodate themselves to varying levels and kinds of inundation.

It was also discovered that the formal model of queue discipline, which admits of medical urgency alone as a preemptive priority, cannot accommodate the fact that a patient's waiting time is also related to his race. And in some classes of hospitals race is about as good a predictor of waiting time as medical urgency. Queue discipline is therefore not fully described independently of its informal properties.[11]

Given the effects of inundation and nonacute medical status, we still face the question of why the Negro patient is discriminated against at all. We may dispose of the two accounts that come most immediately to mind. Because the percentage of blacks among the nonurgent patients is similar regardless of the level of demand on an emergency room (see table 16), racial composition of clientele cannot account for the pattern we have observed.[12] As to the question of whether there might be more prejudiced staffs in the biggest and most congested departments, we can only say that because these larger units are more likely to be associated with medical schools, to be supplied with the latest equipment and employ the most specialists, just the opposite conclusion might be warranted: that the larger facilities are manned by the most professional staffs and exhibit the most racial discrimination in spite of this. But whatever the true differences in staff tendencies in the two groups of emergency rooms, we observe variation in differential treatment *within* the inundated group, for which the invocation of prejudice alone would be an insufficient account.

The data would seem to suggest that, whatever its nature,

attitudinal discrimination requires a unique combination of organizational and medical contingencies if it is to find significant expression on the behavioral level. "Need" and "opportunity" appear to be the basic conditioning elements. In the smaller, less congested facilities, there is no need to impose priorities because demand is so limited. And under high levels of demand, acute ailments must be processed quickly, no matter who presents them, for to do otherwise is to invite scandal and professional sanction. However, those with non-acute disorders who have no legitimate business in the inundated facility are apparently fair game for discriminatory practice. Inundated emergency systems thus furnish the occasion where "need" and "opportunity" for discrimination intersect.

If this argument has any merit at all, then we should expect to find not only racial discrimination but discrimination of any kind to be most pronounced among nonurgent patients in congested systems. This was found to be the case. In a separate analysis, we computed the joint effects on waiting time of all social status indicators—age, sex, marital status, education, and insurance—controlling on everything else, including race. The resulting multiple partial correlation coefficients in the smallest facilities are .07 and .08 among the least and most urgent, respectively. Even in the largest emergency departments the comparable coefficient for the most urgent cases is no higher (.08). Among those who bring nonurgent complaints to inundated facilities, however, the multiple partial correlation coefficient is .26, over three times larger than any of the other three values. Though the differences are somewhat less pronounced, these data clearly reproduce the pattern found for racial discrimination, which is to say that racial bias occurs within a condition that admits of the expression of bias of any kind.

If the intersection of congestion and nonurgency stands as a necessary condition for the activation of race as an allocation criterion, it still does not answer the question of why the *black* should be assigned the inferior priority. Within the limits we have just described, the explanation with the most immediate appeal is latent "racism"; that is to say, the survival of traditional, caste-related attitudes in modern medical institutions. Presupposing some form of racial prejudice to be an aspect of the psychological makeup of emergency room staffs, this explanation accounts for at least part of the independent race effects we have observed and is consistent with their invariant direction. However, the power of this sort of account is attenuated by a number of facts.

First, we must point out that the present study was undertaken during an era that bore witness to a striking increase in the use of emergency departments. This is the case on the local as well as the national level. In 1960, for example, there were 754,428 emergency visits to Cook County hospitals; by 1970 this figure had almost doubled by rising to 1,474,590. At least part of this increase is due to a growing tendency on the part of the general population to make use of emergency facilities, which is reflected in an 82 percent increase from 1960 to 1969 in visits per 1,000 county population. "The single most important factor associated with this increase," according to Gibson, Anderson, and Bugbee (1970: 4–5), "has been the growing numbers of patients being treated for nonemergent medical conditions."

Another point that bears mention is that the largest emergency rooms serve the highest proportion of walk-in patients with minor or chronic disorders.[13] As a result, the organizations best equipped to administer specialized, high quality trauma care tend to be those which are most frequently called upon to provide the least specialized primary care. Of course, the high absolute percentage of walk-in patients is a problem to which no emergency room staff is indifferent. Doctors do not like being used as substitutes or stand-ins for out-patient departments. In addition, they resent having to perform tasks which are inconsistent with their conception of "what they are *supposed* to do." These troubles are only magnified in the larger emergency departments, whose typically lower staff-patient ratios lead to greater congestion and attending disorder per unit increase in demand—a new fact which superimposes upon primary medical care a waiting room policing function.

The above dilemma is tied into the matter of race. For the total sample, a higher proportion of blacks are found among walk-ins than among bona fide emergencies. Of all "emergent" cases only 28.6 percent are black; the percentage black among the "urgent" is 32 percent; and for the "nonurgent" this figure rises to 46.8 percent. On the face of it, of course, these statistics could have nothing to do with the race effects we have observed, for these were computed with urgency-level controlled. However, we must appreciate the precise meaning of what we have and have not accomplished by doing so.

By partialing the relationship between race and waiting time on urgency, we deliberately adjust for the relationship between urgency and race. But this procedure only controls for the "objective" side of the latter relationship; it may not negate its "subjective" effects. That is to say, the statistical operation may fail to eliminate the adverse *reputational* consequences of the relationship. Accordingly, the black patient who appears in an emergency room for treatment of a nonurgent problem may not simply be viewed as a patient with a minor problem but as the *kind of patient who brings minor problems to the emergency room*. If this is so, then issue will be made of the social characteristics of the patient as well as his physical condition. Within inundated facilities, this double "stigma"—illegitimate complaint and unworthy social character (i.e., membership in a group that "causes trouble")—finds expression in a double delay (57.6 minutes, as opposed to 17.5 to 24.0 minutes for all other categories).

This interpretation suggests that the inferior priority assigned to individual black patients may stem less from staff's *psychological* inclinations toward bigotry than from the concrete *organizational* problems that are "caused" by the black as a *social category*. This account is consistent with the disproportionate race effect that is found among nonurgent cases in congested facilities. Only when he needlessly burdens the system, then, will the black patient be significantly discriminated against.

An additional bit of evidence may be brought to bear in this respect. If the association between race and urgency generates reputational import that disproportionately delays nonurgent blacks, then that association should be more pronounced in the group in which the delay due to race is greatest. This expectation conforms to our data. Whereas the proportion of blacks in the least congested emergency rooms is 13 percent higher among the least urgent than among the more urgent cases, the comparable percentage difference in the larger and more congested facilities is 26 percent (see table 16). Thus, the stronger the association between urgency and race, the more pronounced the effect of race on waiting time—even when that effect is statistically partialed on urgency.

We must hasten to admit that however well founded they may be, the above considerations do not deny the possibility of real prejudice, which may ensure the adverse reputational implications that might be completely overlooked in its absence. But though we may indeed be faced with a form of racism, it is by no means a simple, personal kind; rather it seems to be an attitude that is intensified and perhaps in part created by organizational problems. Rationalizeable in terms of a legitimate concern for emergency room efficiency, this brand of racial discrimination differs from that which is based upon traditional, caste-related beliefs—although the more subtle kinds of prejudice may be superimposed upon a primitive kind rather than replace it. However this may be, the fact that a patient's race will not affect his priority when a complaint is bona fide—even in congested facilities—suggests that when objectives of unquestionable salience govern medical activities, discrimination will be almost totally eliminated, whether personal prejudice be present or not.

Taken together, the statistical findings reported here seem to confirm Roth's (1972: 849) observations, which were drawn from ethnographic studies of six public and private hospital emergency departments in the northeastern and western United States:

> The negative evaluation of patients is strongest when they combine an undeserving character with illegitimate demands. Thus, a patient presenting a minor medical complaint at an inconvenient hour is more vigorously condemned if he is a welfare case than if he is a "respectable citizen." On the other hand, a "real emergency" can overcome moral repugnance. Thus, when a presumed criminal suffering a severe abdominal bullet wound inflicted by police was brought into an emergency ward, the staff quickly mobilized in a vigorous effort to prevent death because this is the kind of case the staff sees as justifying the existence of their unit. The same patient brought in with a minor injury would almost certainly have been treated as a moral outcast.

As far as the policy implications of this research are concerned, there are really only two issues. The first is whether the inferior priority assigned to nonurgent black patients is mostly due to race as such or to the fact that blacks *as a category* tend to make improper use of the emergency system. What is not at issue are the congestion and inefficiency that stem from improper utilization. A second issue is whether the longer delay reserved for undeserving *black* patients subverts or enhances the efficiency of the emergency service system by discouraging improper use, making available more time and energy to and allowing greater priority for bona fide patients of *both races*. If the answer to this question is an affirmative one, then we may conclude that the inferior priority assigned to undeserving blacks very much lends itself to the formal objective of the emergency unit, which is to provide fast, efficient and impersonal treatment to all those who need it. This is of course to attribute a positive function to discrimination by urgency, not race. On the other hand, the argument does not recommend relief for blacks, but, instead, a more stringent.rationing of priority for whites.

But this is far from an optimal solution. The recommendation to seek means to control the discretion of servers in the allocation of priority could only be advanced out of a sense of moral indignation at the discovery of bias among emergency department personnel. Such counsel implies that effectiveness of medical care consists, in part, of its vicissitudes being independent of the social origins of those to whom it is administered. But this is a most questionable objective for emergency room policy; for, when we look precisely into the matter, we see that racial bias occurs only in the treatment of persons who have no business in the emergency room in the first place. To recommend that bias be eliminated among the illegitimate is to set down a line of action to which we would all agree in principle but which in the present case is functionally irrelevant because it concerns a population that belongs in a different kind of medical facility. So far as its practice is limited to this population, racial discrimination comes into view as the system's danger signal, a warning that something is wrong organizationally, not psychologically. There seems to be no doubt as to the source of difficulty: it is an admissions policy that fails to screen out inappropriate clientele in inundated systems. Far from being a contributing cause of this problem, racial discrimination is one of its consequences, which is to be remedied by reorganization rather than by more effective constraints on queue discipline within existing emergency department frameworks.

3   The Meaning of Waiting

6 Waiting, Deference, and Distributive Justice

> Wasting the time of any businessman is equivalent to robbing his wallet. Keeping him waiting is bad business practice and bad manners.
> [If a delay is inevitable], your secretary should explain the circumstances and ask him if he would mind waiting. She might ask him into your private office, take his coat and hat, see that he is seated and comfortable. She might ask him if he would like her to get him a magazine to read, or coffee or tea, or a soft drink while he is waiting for you.
> This is routine in many organizations.
>
> Milla Alihan, *Corporate Etiquette*

Deference is that component of activity by which one person expresses his appreciation of the social value of another in face-to-face interaction with him. Deferential gestures have long been thought to be central to the maintenance of organized social relationships (Spencer 1886). However, while there has been recent progress in the delineation of types of deference (Goffman 1956) and identification of the social attributes with which its varying expressions are associated (Shils 1970), we have up to now no empirical knowledge of the *principles* which govern the way deference is allocated in social systems. The purpose of the present investigation is to address this problem by assessing the validity of one distributional model.

Our basic hypothesis is that deference is allocated according to the principle of distributive justice; however, when more than one kind of deferential act is available, the resulting distribution violates this principle. We shall try to show that

The data on which this chapter is based were collected by Caroline Wolf.

injustice in the apportionment of deference does not stem from deviation from rules of just exchange but is rather an inevitable consequence of conforming to them. This hypothesis will be tested with data relating to waiting time in a private bureaucracy.

Waiting as a Factor in Social Exchange

To be delayed is usually a source of irritation to a person because it increases the investment he must make in order to obtain a service, thereby increasing its cost and reducing the profit to be derived from it. This loss is related to the fact that time is a finite resource whose use implies a renunciation of other activities. Thus, what is expended in a waiting room or in some other waiting channel is not unused time at all but, rather, used time, in the form of more rewarding interaction foregone.

In the framework of social exchange, rewards find their functional referent in the offsetting of costs (Homans 1961: 61-64). In this investigation we shall study two kinds of concrete rewards: (1) the offering of a beverage by a secretary to a waiting client and (2) the personal escort that an executive provides this same person. These forms of "remedial deference" (Goffman 1971: 95-187) may be counterposed to the costs that clients incur in waiting.

Distributive Justice

Although waiting subtracts from the profitability of a relationship, it cannot be said that identical amounts of waiting entail identical costs. For, in occupying more or less important statuses and providing differentially skilled and available services, the time of some clients must be considered to be more valuable (from a purely social and/or economic standpoint) than the time of others. This being so, compensatory modes must be calibrated to the worth as well as the amount of client-time lost through waiting—which is to propose that, in waiting rooms, perceived value of a client's time is what makes his social rank a "deference-entitling property" (Shils 1970: 422). This expectation is in accord with the rule of *distributive justice*, which dictates that rewards (whether material or symbolic) be commensurate with both costs and investments. Homans (1971: 75) expresses himself in this regard as follows: "A man in an exchange relation with another will expect that the rewards of each man be proportional to his costs—the greater the rewards, the greater the costs—and that the net rewards, or profits, of each man be proportional to his investments—the greater the investments, the greater the profit."

The amount of time a client waits represents a cost to him; the value of the time lost reflects his investments. As Blau (1964a: 194) puts it, "Quite aside from the direct costs in time and energy required for supplying benefits in exchange for others, the supply of certain benefits depends also on having previously invested resources in the capacity to supply them." The investment thus enters into the exchange equation as an additional cost. Accordingly, if two clients expend the same amount of time in the waiting room, the one having made the superior investments (indexed by his social rank) should receive the greater rewards. To coordinate rewards with waiting time is therefore to merely offset the *costs* of delay; the coordination of rewards with social rank is to recognize superior *investments* and grant them their due.

Homans' discussion of "status congruence" (1961: 240) brings to expression another closely related implication. "Apparently, distributive justice demands not just that higher investment should receive higher reward in one respect but that it should do so in all." This would lead us to expect different forms of accommodative deference to be directed toward the very same persons. That *justice* should demand this, however, is surely open to question. A person might simply use superior rewards presently conferred to gain further benefits. Blau, in fact, suggests that "If the rule of justice is . . . that profits should be proportional to investments, the multiplication of social profits implicit in the strain toward status congruence violates this rule." The rule may in other words carry within itself its own contradiction: If two or more rewards are allocated on the basis of the same costs and investments, then individuals will accumulate benefits without accumulating deficits. But there is another side to the matter. In some instances, no single reward can offset the costs that an individual may incur; therefore, an *accumulation* of rewards will be necessary to satisfy the requirements of equitable exchange. The justice of status congruence is therefore an empirical question.

Hypotheses

The theory of distributive justice admits of the following inferences with respect to costs, investments, rewards, and the relationships between them.

1. Those who incur the greatest costs in an exchange relationship will receive a greater measure of reward *per unit investment* than persons who incur the lesser costs.

2. In addition to the coordination of costs and rewards, distributive justice demands that profits (rewards less costs) be proportional to investments. This means that persons who have made the greater investments must receive a greater measure of reward *per unit cost* incurred than those who have made the lesser investments.

3. Whatever the measure of reward, costs and investments must be inversely related to one another. That is, people with the greater investments should incur less cost *per unit reward* they receive.

4. Different kinds of rewards will promote status congruence by being allocated to the same kinds of people. Distributive justice requires that this relationship reflect the greater value of the costs and investments of these same people; otherwise, their rewards and profits will feed into and subserve one another independently of their outlays and so contradict this exchange model. In more formal terms, distributive justice will be realized if a zero relationship obtains between any two rewards when costs and investments are controlled; if such a relationship exceeds zero, then status congruence may be said to be inconsistent with just exchange. For this would mean that rewards are being accumulated without a corresponding increase in outlays.

In this investigation, cost is indexed by waiting time, investment by client status, and rewards by deferential drink-offering and escort.

These indices are mundane enough in their content; however, the theoretical relationships between the terms to which they relate are stated at a level which is independent of content. Distributive justice is thus a general theory of the way social systems allocate the rewards at their disposal. If this is so, then by inquiring into the allocative mechanism of the microcosmic waiting room setting, we can learn something about macrocosmic orders. The rules that govern what we give and get in a small way can thus tell us what to expect when the stakes are higher.

Before proceeding, a prefatory remark must be made. While the above hypotheses make specific reference to the direction in which rewards must be allocated if the resulting apportionment is to conform to the requirements of distributive justice, they are ambiguous as to intentional mode, leaving open the question of whether diffusion of deference is effected by deliberate action or whether the culminating distribution is an unintentional one. The contrast between these modalities defines what is at stake in a confirmation of the hypotheses. If these hypotheses are in fact *descriptions* of an existing policy, then the measure of their support would index the extent to which that policy has been implemented. If, on the other hand, there are neither formal nor tacitly recognized rules, nor consciously differential motivation concerning the treatment of waiting clients, then we may assume that the deference actions reported in this investigation are for the most part governed by a principle of which the participants themselves are unaware. While neither of these models perfectly fits the reality of the situation, it is our opinion that the latter model, emphasizing the unwitting nature of the exchange process, is the one which captures this reality most adequately.

Research Setting

The site of our research is the executive office of a mortgage company located in an eastern American city. Activities of the firm have as their objective the financing and exchanging of real (commercial) property for profit. This end is pursued within a very highly competitive market.

The executive office itself is stratified in an unambiguous way. At the top of the hierarchy are the chairman and vice-chairman of the board. Below them are two presidents, each governing a separate division of the company; the third stratum consists of two senior vice-presidents. Subject to these high-level executives are three vice-presidents and two assistant vice-presidents. These positions exhaust the executive stratum, to which an eight man professional staff is subject. Finally, nine secretaries, an office girl, and a receptionist constitute the bottom of the office hierarchy.

The Waiting Room

Those who have occasion to meet with a member of this firm must first enter a waiting room, which is situated at the office's main entrance. Because of the frequency and timing of clients' visits, this area is never congested. Very rarely, in fact, are the clients of more than one executive found there at any one time.

The atmosphere of the waiting room is contemporary and plush. Furnishings are fancy and include fine paneling and dark brown carpeting. The receptionist's territory, comprising a reception desk and switchboard, stands out in white. For the clients there are four apparently expensive chairs arranged in sets of two, between each of which is a coffee table supplied with an ashtray and telephone. There is also a supply of *The Wall Street Journal* and *Barron's*, and magazines, including the *New Yorker* and *Fortune*. Information about the company is available in the form of mortgage investment quarterly reports and prospectuses. On the wall are trophies: framed pictures of some of the company's biggest real estate deals.

Data Collection

Data were collected by one of the investigators during her employment as a receptionist. Observations were made during the regular course of her work, unbeknown to anyone else in the organization. The co-investigator's status as participant observer allowed her to record in an unobtrusive fashion patterns and nuances of behavior which most certainly would have been altered had her research function been known.

Fifty-two consecutive observations were made over a six week period and were recorded in the following manner. After a client announced himself and the name of the executive with whom he had an appointment, the time of his arrival and title of his host were recorded on a small card. The client's behavior during the waiting period was also recorded. Included were his phone calls and his reception by the secretary of the executive he was to see, who may or may not have offered him refreshment. It was also possible to make note of the client's demeanor, the way he occupied himself as he waited, remarks to the receptionist, and so forth. When an executive was ready to meet with him, the observer noted whether the client was escorted into the office by the executive himself, his secretary, or just told to go in alone after having been given directions by the receptionist. The time at which he was invited in for his appointment was also noted, so that a fairly precise estimate of waiting time could be entered on his card.

We should make it clear that the unit of analysis for our tabulations is the appointment, not the client. This specification is required by the fact that in twelve instances (almost 24 percent of all observations) a group of two or more people was to be seen by a single executive. The necessary accounting rule was simply that a quantifiable act toward any member is attributed to the unit. This procedure paralleled the deference rule: never was beverage or escort offered to one member of a group and denied to others.

Our sample does not include all who entered the waiting room. Omitted are pedestrians in search of a bathroom, messengers, delivery men, clients seeking an audience with one of the secretaries, and clients of non-executives, of which there were but two.

Assumptions

We were unfortunately not able to obtain direct information on clients' statuses—which is an important weakness in our data and a shortcoming that was quite impossible to overcome. For the receptionist to have questioned a client about his organizational affiliation, much less his position within that organization, would have been an unheard-of violation of corporate etiquette. And to request information on clients from the executives themselves was equally unthinkable.

Yet there is good reason to believe that clients who have dealings with those at the top of another company's executive hierarchy very probably hold an equally important position in their own organization. Being responsible for corporate policy, top executives must have direct or indirect contact with their own subordinates in order to obtain the data on which a policy is to be based and to see to its execution, once formulated; however, there is no functional rationale for contact between policymakers of one organization and those who inform or execute the policy of another. Accordingly, contacts *between* companies must be undertaken by persons holding similar positions, since the formation of agreements presupposes the coming together of those with the authority to make them. The implementation of agreements requires meetings among lesser executives, who discuss and work out the details.

The assumption of a direct relationship between client and executive rank may be supported on empirical as well as theoretical grounds. To begin with, we observed a very definite difference in the way clients of higher and lower-level executives presented themselves. The first group was an older one and distinctly more self-assured; there was in addition an air of busyness about them that was absent in the more casual second group. For instance, many among the top executives' clients expressed impatience at not being seen at once; some tried to go directly to the office of the person with whom they had an appointment, only to be asked by his secretary to return to the waiting room and remain there until called; other clients at first refused to take off their coat and sit down, as if such a gesture might symbolize resignation to accept a loss they were not willing to bear. Secondly, these clients expected to be well-treated and accepted the firm's hospitality as a matter of course. One afternoon, for example, the office girl passed through the waiting room in order to get herself a soda from the outside vending machine. On passing back through, she was confronted by a client, who took the drink from her hand with thanks, assuming it was for him. Clients of low-level executives would not as a rule have been so presumptuous. These relatively young men are in fact characterized by a demeanor quite opposite to that exhibited by their superiors; they are impressed by their hosts and are visibly moved by whatever is done for them. They are the people who are willing to wait and to content themselves in their own way until seen.

To be sure, there is no way to show conclusively that executive and client ranks are highly correlated; yet, reason and evidence very pointedly justify the assumption that they are.

Data preparation. A limited number of observations caused us to dichotomize the client rank and waiting time variables. The waiting time distribution was split just before the whole number which immediately followed its median value; that is, between five and six minutes. A client was classified in terms of the rank of the executive with whom he had an appointment. Officials who held a senior vice-presidential or higher rank were placed in the top executive category; vice-presidents and assistant vice-presidents were defined as low-level executives. This division corresponds to what seems to us to be a "natural break" in the real distribution of power and responsibility within the firm. In addition, this breaking point divides the client rank order as close to its median as possible.

Results
Client Rank and Waiting Time

Because of the relatively greater value of their time, higher ranked clients lose most by being kept waiting; on this account, waiting time and rank (representing costs and investments, respectively) must be inversely related if distributive justice is to be realized. The data in table 17 indicate that waiting time and client rank are *directly* associated.

TABLE 17.   Relationship between Executive Rank and Client Waiting Time

| | Rank of Executive | | | | | |
| | High-level | | Low-level | | Total | |
Client waiting time[a]	%	No.	%	No.	%	No.
Short	36	(10)	75	(18)	46	(28)
Long	64	(18)	25	(6)	54	(24)
Total	100	(28)	100	(24)	100	(52)

[a]Waiting time is short when it is five minutes or less, long when it is six minutes or more.

There is no ambiguity in this relationship. Among clients waiting to see members of the top of the executive hierarchy, 64 percent are delayed for more than five minutes, compared to only 25 percent of clients having appointments with lesser executives. At the other end of the distribution, 75 percent of the lower-rank clients wait *less* than five minutes while only 36 percent of the more important people are delayed for so short a time.[1] The direction of this relationship maintains itself within each of the two dichotomous reward categories: drink-offering (see table 18) and escort (see table 19).[2] Hypothesis 3, which predicts that people with the greater investments incur less cost for the rewards they receive, is therefore contradicted.[3]

However, these data do not in themselves constitute grounds for denying the constraint of distributive justice. While the object of this test is an inference from that principle, namely, the tendency for waiting time to be suppressed among the most important and powerful clientele, the result in table 17 seems to reflect the tendency for important and powerful *executives* to keep their clients waiting the longest. This is probably because the superordinate official is instrumental to the ends of so many people that anyone who desires his service cannot gain immediate access to him but must wait until others are accommodated. Accessibility is thus affected by the status of a server as well as his client. This means that the profitability of an exchange depends upon the supply of a reward (in this case, a service) in relation to its collective demand as well as the individual investments which may be brought to bear with a view to its acquisition. The formulations of distributive justice must therefore presuppose constancy of supply and demand, which cannot be satisfied in the present case, where subordinate executives are more accessible than superordinate executives. (In this connection, see Abrahamsson 1970.)

The Drink Offering

If servers are unable to see their clients immediately, then those who manage service systems can keep on hand ritual supplies, like drinks, which are freely bestowed in order to ensure the comfort of a client while he waits. But if drink offerings also served a specifically compensatory[4] function, we would expect the frequency with which they are bestowed to be directly related to waiting time. To the objection that longer waiting periods allow greater opportunity to serve a beverage, we can only say that offerings are not randomly distributed across a waiting period but rather bestowed at its outset by a secretary who knows how long the recipient is going to be delayed. We may point out, however, that the offering is apparently made with a view to providing comfort, not compensation. That it may be a function of the offering does not therefore lend to compensation a motivational status.

Table 18 shows that regardless of the rank of his appointment, the probability of a client's being subject to a deferential drink offering increases with the time he spends in the waiting room.

TABLE 18.   Relationship between Beverage Offer, Executive Rank, and Client Waiting Time

Beverage offer	Rank of Executive					
	High-level		Low-level		Total	
	%	No.	%	No.	%	No.
Short waiting time						
Beverage offered	20	(2)	6	(1)	11	(3)
Beverage not offered	80	(8)	94	(17)	89	(25)
Total	100	(10)	100	(18)	100	(28)
Long waiting time						
Beverage offered	44	(8)	17	(1)	38	(9)
Beverage not offered	56	(10)	83	(5)	62	(15)
Total	100	(18)	100	(6)	100	(24)
Totals						
Beverage offered	36	(10)	8	(2)	23	(12)
Beverage not offered	64	(18)	92	(22)	77	(40)
Total	100	(28)	100	(24)	100	(52)

The portion of clients to whom this gesture is accorded increases from 11 to 38 percent during the earliest and latest parts of a waiting hour. The corresponding figures for high-level clients are 20 and 44 percent; for low-level clients, 6 and 17 percent. These findings are consistent with hypothesis 1, which states that deferential rewards will be directly related to waiting time, in view of its costs, which increase as time passes.

As can also be seen in table 18, 36 percent of the top executives' clients were offered a beverage, with a corresponding figure of only 8 percent for lesser clientele. While it is the former who experience the longest delays, the direction of this relationship is maintained in each waiting-time interval, with the more worthy clients being in all cases more than twice as likely to be offered refreshment. Thus, among those who wait less than six minutes, 20 percent of high-level executives' clients are served a drink; 6 percent of the lesser clients are so honored. Comparable percentages in the longer waiting period are 44 and 17 percent.

While the relationship between waiting time and drink offering gives independent expression to a service system's "recognition" of a minimal level of deference to which all clients are entitled by virtue of the costs incurred in waiting, the relationship between client status and beverage offer, being independent of waiting time, indicates perception of the differential level of clients' investments.[5] It shows that by the selective granting and withholding of a deferential offering, a service system can affirm and celebrate the differential value of clients' time. The findings in table 18 thus confirm hypothesis 2, which predicts a direct and independent relationship between a client's investments and the amount of reward allotted to him.[6]

"Rites of Passage"

Up to this point, we have devoted ourselves to a deference gesture accorded and received within the waiting room. We now inquire into the way ceremonial appreciation of clients' worth is expressed in connection with passage into the service facility.

In the present organization there are at least three patterns of escort. An executive may enter the waiting room himself and personally lead a client into his office; or he may cause a representative (his secretary) to act as an escort; or he may order the receptionist to give a client directions on how to find the way into his office. By delegating the responsibility for escort to another, the executive may continue to devote himself to exclusively *technical* pursuits; however, by taking this function upon himself he celebrates the presence of his own client and so becomes implicated in the *ceremonial* sphere. It is in this sense that different forms of escort correspond to differing levels of symbolic appreciation of both a client's personal merit and the costs that he has incurred through having been delayed.

If the principles which govern passage from one part of a service system to the next derive from the very rules which regulate accords within the waiting room, then we would expect the deference-entitling properties of their statuses to differentiate among clients' escorts according to the rule of distributive justice. Table 19 tends to confirm this expectation.

We constructed this table by counting the number of times clients were escorted into an executive's office by the incumbent himself, as against the frequency with which they were self-escorted, after having been given directions, or escorted by the executive's secretary. Our results show that of the clients having appointments with high-level executives, 75 percent were

TABLE 19.   Relationship between Escort Behavior, Executive Rank, and Client Waiting Time

Escort	Rank of Executive					
	High-level		Low-level		Total	
	%	No.	%	No.	%	No.
Short waiting time						
Executive	50	(5)	33	(6)	39	(11)
Secretary or self-escorted	50	(5)	67	(12)	61	(17)
Total	100	(10)	100	(18)	100	(28)
Long waiting time						
Executive	89	(16)	33	(2)	75	(18)
Secretary or self-escorted	11	(2)	67	(4)	25	(6)
Total	100	(18)	100	(6)	100	(24)
Totals						
Executive	75	(21)	33	(8)	56	(29)
Secretary or self-escorted	25	(7)	67	(16)	44	(23)
Total	100	(28)	100	(24)	100	(52)

personally escorted by the executive, as opposed to 33 percent of those less worthy clients who had appointments with their subordinates.

There are at least two plausible reasons for this pattern. First, higher-level executives may be housed in offices that are nearer to the waiting room than the offices of their inferiors. This is indeed the case, but with one fortunate exception which helps us to assess the merit of the argument. That exception is one of the senior vice-presidents, who is located as far away from the waiting room as any of his subordinates, and even farther than some. In a separate analysis, however, we found that this official personally escorted all of his clients, as compared to his inferiors, who escorted only a third of theirs. Even beyond this datum, however, the proximity theory seems rather far-fetched when taken at face value, for while there are differences in physical distance between the waiting room and the various offices, these are really a matter of several feet and could hardly add up to much in terms of bother or inconvenience. Indeed, if the offices of the lower-level executives were significantly less accessible than those of their superiors, we would expect a smaller proportion of their clients to be *self-escorted*, which another separate analysis shows not to be the case.

It is the theory of distributive justice, not proximity, which provides the most credible account of the pattern found in table 19. As we have already noted, the distributive equilibrium upset by keeping an important person waiting can be restored by the executive's deferential offering of himself as that person's escort. While this assumption is consistent with the hypothesized direct relationship between rewards and investments, another test of the restorative function of executive escort would require that it be associated with waiting time among similarly statused executives, in accordance with hypothesis 1: those who incur the greatest costs will receive the greater measure of reward per unit investment. The results of both tests are shown in the body of table 19.

These data partially disconfirm the latter hypothesis by showing the escort behavior of inferior executives, which occurs 33 percent of the time in both the shortest and longest waiting time intervals, to be unresponsive to client delay. For top executives, personal escort adheres to a different pattern, increasing from 50 percent in the shortest waiting time interval to 89 percent in the longest. In addition, the result shows that major clients are more likely to receive executive escort, no matter how long they have been kept waiting. Half of the high ranking clients, as opposed to a third of the low ranking clients, are escorted by their appointments in the shorter waiting period; in the longer period, the corresponding percentages are 89 and 33. This finding further confirms hypothesis 2.

The Relationship Between "Waiting Rites" and "Passage Rites": A Measure of Status Congruence

We have treated two separate kinds of remedial gestures connected with waiting time: those deferentially accorded clients (1) during their stay in the waiting room and (2) during their movement from the waiting room to the executive office. We have, then, rites associated with waiting and rites associated with passage. Both, we found, are practiced in a way that generally conforms to the rule of distributive justice, with the most deference being allocated to those whose waiting entailed the most cost (taking into account, of course, the differential value of clients' time). If these two ceremonial patterns are to be construed as interlocking aspects of a broader ritual system that is governed by the same principle which regulates its parts, we

should expect waiting rites to be predictive of passage rites—
and so reflect clients' status congruence in a way that contradicts the principle of distributive justice, which requires that
deferential rewards be independent, given specific levels of
cost and investment. Table 20 shows that covariation among
deference forms is maintained regardless of the level of either
kind of outlay.

TABLE 20.   Relationship between Escort Behavior, Beverage Offer, and
Client Waiting Time

Escort	Beverage offered to client		Beverage not offered to client		Total	
	%	No.	%	No.	%	No.
Short waiting time						
Executive	67	(2)	36	(9)	39	(11)
Secretary or self-escorted	33	(1)	64	(16)	61	(17)
Total	100	(3)	100	(25)	100	(28)
Long waiting time						
Executive	89	(8)	67	(10)	75	(18)
Secretary or self-escorted	11	(1)	33	(5)	25	(6)
Total	100	(9)	100	(15)	100	(24)
Rank of executive: high-level						
Executive	90	(9)	67	(12)	75	(21)
Secretary or self-escorted	10	(1)	33	(6)	25	(7)
Total	100	(10)	100	(18)	100	(28)
Rank of executive: low-level						
Executive	50	(1)	32	(7)	33	(8)
Secretary or self-escorted	50	(1)	68	(15)	67	(16)
Total	100	(2)	100	(22)	100	(24)
Totals						
Executive	83	(10)	48	(19)	56	(29)
Secretary or self-escorted	17	(2)	52	(21)	44	(23)
Total	100	(12)	100	(40)	100	(52)

Even though an executive rarely or never knows whether a
drink offering has been bestowed by his secretary, he tends to
put himself in the position of escort for clients who have been
so treated. Looking at the bottom or summary portion of table
20, we find that 83 percent of those initially offered a beverage
in the waiting room are later escorted into the service facility by
the executive himself, as opposed to 48 percent of those who
received no such initial offer. This pattern is not to be explained

in terms of waiting time, even though both practices are related to it. Thus, within the shortest waiting interval, 67 percent of the clients offered a drink later received executive escort; of those not served, only 36 percent were so escorted. Comparable figures for the longest interval are 89 and 67 percent.

The above pattern is also maintained when client rank is introduced as a test variable. Among clients of top executives, 90 percent of the beverage recipients and 67 percent of the non-recipients later receive personal escort. For those awaiting low-level executives the corresponding figures are 50 and 32 percent.

Because they make manifest the tendency for rewards to outstrip costs and investments, these data are consistent with the proposition that distributive justice contains a dynamic by means of which it contradicts itself: Controlling for costs and investments does *not* negate the association between rewards. This is to say that rewards may be accumulated independently of outlays. This outcome is consistent with the tendency toward status congruence, which, in turn, violates distributive justice, the very principle from which it derives.[7]

Summary

Distributive justice is a theory which holds that in social affairs rewards (whether material or symbolic) are allocated on the basis of costs *and* investments. The costs to which this investigation was addressed were indexed by the waiting period; investments were reflected in the differential status of clients; the rewards studied were deferentially accommodative in nature.

Our analysis focused on a service system located in a competitive exchange structure, to which many of its characteristics may be related. Above all, this organization is subject to the principle that the greater the competition among social units, the more salient to its clients do small differences among them become. Because the amount of time a client spends waiting represents a cost to him (part of the price of doing business, so to say), that time will be of great salience when it is one of the few factors which differentiate one service organization from another. But in any organization there are randomly and systematically occurring contingencies to which an execu-

tive is subject which prevent him from seeing a client immediately; for this reason, a competitive service system must, at
the time it causes a wait, build in procedures that compensate
for having done so. Like individuals (Goffman 1971; 113), it is as
if an organization can split itself in half, one part considering
itself blameworthy for the delay of its clients; the other,
renouncing that offense and, in a number of real and symbolic
ways, indemnifying them for their loss. The firm that we studied
offset its delaying tendencies by providing waiting facilities that
were striking in their beauty and convenience, a holding area
not only worthy of the very important people that it accom-
modates but one which must also allow whomever it receives to
feel most worthy.

But just as one competitive service system must try to outdo
others in providing agreeable waiting room accommodations, so
it must outdo itself in providing better treatment for some
clients than for others,[8] in accordance with the differential value
of their time. Such an operation is made possible by a common
definition of worthiness, arrived at no doubt through repeated
experience with different types of clients, that allows executives
and their secretaries[9] to fit their lines of action toward a client
together so as to build up or produce a recurrent, predictable
pattern of joint deferential action. This pattern finds expression
in very definite statistical relationships between waiting time,
beverage offer, and modalities of escort.[10] On a structural level,
these relationships reflect a ceremonial system of interlocking
compensatory rites.

It bears repeating that coordination of separate lines of action
is an unintentional achievement based on a definition of worth
to which this pattern may not be reduced, even though all
parties may be committed to it. As such, the ceremonial system
to which this definition gives rise is an emergent form, an
unanticipated consequence of a principle that, as if by an
"invisible hand," governs the conduct of *individuals*. This is
confirmed by the statistical, as opposed to deterministic, nature
of the relationships we have observed. If variations in the
treatment of clients were really intentional—that is, preformu-
lated as policy—then deference gestures would be totally
predictable, given knowledge of clients' status. That this is
patently not the case reflects the unintentional nature of the

system herein described. It is precisely because of its lack of explicit formulation that deference patterns are subject to extraneous effects which suppress their statistical expression to a level well below unity.

Within this limit, hypotheses 1 and 2, which predict costs and investments to be independent criteria for the allocation of rewards, were almost consistently confirmed. The other two hypotheses were rejected in such a manner as to help clarify the boundary within which the theory of distributive justice must be confined. In this investigation, costs and investments were found to be directly rather than inversely related to one another (as predicted in hypothesis 3) because the supply-demand ratio differed among top and low-level executives. We therefore concluded that distributive justice holds within narrow rather than broad limits of supply and demand. We also discovered that the different kinds of rewards a client receives will feed into and subserve one another independently of his costs and investments. This outcome contradicts hypothesis 4, which predicts the kind of status congruence that obtains when the allocation of different modalities of reward reflect the greater value of the outlays of those who receive them. Actually, the very integration of deference gestures presupposes that this not be so. A deference system, defined as an organization of integrated compensatory modes, is incompatible with just exchange because it requires that the reward levels *separately* predicted by distributive justice act back and contradict that rule when considered in the *aggregate*. Distributive justice is in this sense unintentionally violated through the very act of conforming to it. While each server grants a client his proper due, the resulting distribution (effected by two servers) allows some clients somewhat more than their due. The outcome thus accords with the more ancient and ironic exchange principle, "Unto everyone that hath shall be given, and he shall have abundance: but from him that hath not shall be taken away" (Matt. 25: 29).

7 Religious Variation in Client Impatience

Punctuality is a valued personal characteristic which enters into the analysis of interaction in two ways: as an expectation and as a sense of obligation. Just as we demand promptness of ourselves when we deal with others, so we expect the same of them in their dealings with us; hence the righteous indignation when we are unreasonably delayed. But this inner sentiment has a distinct structural referent. Because its manifest consequence is to minimize delay and resulting congestion on a collective level, the norm of punctuality is a central and indispensable feature of complex urban systems. Far from merely giving expression to idiosyncratic personal traits and tendencies, then, the impatience which presupposes a punctual attitude is a socially patterned sentiment which promotes efficiency in modern society. However, the expression of impatience still exhibits considerable variation within such a society, quite independently of psychological differences.

Impatience may be related to two primary sources. On the one hand, irritation over a delay is typically assumed to be some function of the length of the delay itself; on the other, cultural values from which punctual modes of feeling and acting are derived promote impatience and cause it to vary independently of waiting time. This investigation seeks to identify these cultural sources and to measure their effect. Given that the sociological analysis of delay must include not only generalizations about waiting but also about its *meaning*, this problem takes on a very special significance. Above all, it implies a distinction between the objective and subjective costs of delay—a division which itself suggests that the meaning of waiting is conferred by individuals and is not inherent in waiting as such.

The Meaning of Time and Its Religious Sources

To conceive of waiting as a personal experience or problem is to assume a particular way of conceiving time. One aspect of this conception is the division of time into units that can be reliably measured. The ensuing capacity to define punctuality in a precise way is instrumental to the concrete experience of waiting. Thereby, individuals can understand and feel how long they are delayed; statistical and cultural norms for delay may develop and the behavior of others may be assessed in terms of them. This way of thinking about and experiencing daily affairs was no doubt made possible by the perfection and diffusion of the clock, which itself coincided with the development and spread of the industrial process.[1] However, the availability of accurate timepieces is only a necessary condition of punctuality; an equally important prerequisite seems to be the existence of a generalized ethic which, by demanding full utilization of time (and restrictions on its waste) through reliable and systematic enterprise, exploits the *potential* correlation between chronometry and punctuality.

The compulsion to conduct daily life in a methodical and efficient manner, with particular care as to the use of time, is a tendency profoundly typical of the Protestant attitude. This statement may be documented through a variety of sources. In Protestant theology, for one, we find continual references to the moral preciousness of time. "Keep up a high esteem of time," writes an early Protestant divine, "and be every day more careful that you lose none of your time.... Those that are prodigal of their time despise their own souls" (cited in Weber 1958a: 261). And from a later work by Franklin we read that "*time* is money. He that can earn ten shillings a day by his labour, and goes abroad, or sits idle, one half of that day, though he spends but sixpence during his diversion or idleness, ought not to reckon *that* the only expense; he has really spent, or rather thrown away, five shillings besides" (cited in Weber 1958a: 48).

We may also point to the craft of watchmaking itself, which owes much of its development to the Protestant spirit. It is true that that craft was originally centered in Catholic France. But it is also true that when the Edict of Nantes was revoked, a large number of France's Protestant watchmakers fled to Geneva, the city of Calvin, which then became the time measuring capital of the world. More than we realize, perhaps, the ethic that found its center in that part of the West transformed the rest of it by helping to create the motivational prerequisite for fitting into and refining the time orientation of its age. If this is so, then the pejorative significance of waiting must be deeply rooted in convictions that were at least partly religious in nature and which may still promote time-consciousness and punctuality among those who continue to embrace them.

At bottom, the strenuous antipathy toward idleness so characteristic of Protestant culture is a distinctly irrational one, for it rests upon a belief in the immanent value of activity. How this historically unique assumption came to pass is well-known. In an age of belief, as we may recapitulate Weber's (1958a) account, uncertainty as to predestined election creates a sense of distress for which worldly activity is the only means of remedy. Though Weber could not account for the psychology of this connection, it is known today that compulsive activity or work is a typical response to unbearable states of uncertainty (see, for example, Malinowski 1958: 14; Fromm 1941: 111). What is of course unique about this kind of enterprise is its overdetermination, the fact that one is driven to it by an unconscious moral imperative. The implication of all of this is straightforward: If activity be the greatest virtue, all waste of time becomes the most obnoxious misdeed. "Not leisure and enjoyment," wrote Weber (1958a: 157) "but only activity serves to increase the glory of God. . . . Waste of time is thus the first and in principle deadliest of sins."

This impulse, this revulsion against idleness, seems on at least one level to be tied to its original source. Those *nations* in which punctuality is most valued (i.e., the Scandinavian and German-speaking countries, as well as Great Britain and the United States) are predominantly Protestant. Moreover, the value of punctuality in these societies holds the status of a *general* imperative, infusing social as well as occupational life — as is evidenced by the frequency with which punctuality is positively endorsed and stressed in their modern etiquette manuals. (See, for example, Fenwick 1968; Post 1965; Raymond 1965.)

Such an uncompromising attitude toward time does not seem

to be characteristic of the modern Catholic nations, however. Italy may be taken as one example:

> Italians rarely are on time. . . . Even high government officials show no embarrassment when tardy for appointments and they are unperturbed when others arrive late. . . . [A] nation so casual about punctuality nevertheless displays many clocks in its cities. Besides numerous clocks on buildings, there are sidewalk clocks atop many posts. At one corner of Largo di Torre Argentina in Rome, for example, there are four big clocks within clear view. The fact that these clocks differ by as much as fifteen minutes is of little concern. (Levine 1963: 45)

For an additional account, one may point to the observations of an American traveler who expressed his surprise to find among long Italian queues lighthearted conversation, bantering, and a general air of gaiety. This in contrast to the irritation and sullenness that so plainly characterized their American counterparts.[2] The difference is perhaps intelligible along the lines currently pursued. In the first instance time is external, even irrelevant, to moral self-evaluation; in the latter, the individual is inwardly driven by a motive to account for himself in terms of the use which he makes of time. The diverse meanings of waiting unfold accordingly, finding individual expression in the mood of waiters and collective expression in the climate of queues.

Precisely the same kinds of observations can be made in nearby Greece:

> There are many clocks and watches . . . both in the city and the village. Watches are an important part of a man's trappings, and of a girl's adornment. Clocks are necessary to complete the furnishing of a house. It is not essential as a rule that they run on time or that they run at all. . . . [Thus], when a foreign visitor inquires as to the time of a certain Mass, the subject creates a discussion; and eventually the answer will be something like: "Between 2 and 3." . . . At church [moreover] the people are not impatient while waiting for Mass to begin. (Mead 1955: 71)

The same pattern may be found in the Western hemisphere. For example, those who have traveled to both Mexican and American cities know that *hora mejicana* admits of a greater tolerance of delay than *hora americana*. And in the predominantly Catholic countries of South America, one observer notes that "if you are invited for dinner at 7:00 you can appear then, if you wish, but eat a snack first" (de Grazia 1962: 309).

To be sure, the above accounts do not form a systematic or exhaustive argument; yet, they do at least suggest a relationship between religion and the kind of time-reckoning that lends itself to impatience. We shall now inquire into the extent to which this relationship might manifest itself *within* one modern nation. Specifically, we want to determine whether diverse levels of impatience among clients in a postindustrial society are really embedded in their religious backgrounds. What is at stake in this problem, in its broadest terms, at least, is whether that nation's master institutional processes of urbanization, industrialization and bureaucracy have overcome and homogenized religious differences with respect to a crucial aspect of modern life, or whether these differences continue to exert powerful effects on thinking and feeling in the face of such homogenizing forces.

Data Collection and Measurement

The material used in this investigation is drawn from a nationwide survey related to health care use, expenditures, and opinions conducted by the Center for Health Administration Studies and the National Opinion Research Center of the University of Chicago. Data were gathered in 1971 and cover 2,851 heads of households throughout the United States. The survey included a general and health opinion questionnaire, both of which were administered to the head of the household. These instruments are the main sources of information for this report.

The sample itself was designed (for reasons having nothing to do with this investigation) to include a disproportionate number of inner city poor and rural families, as well as more elderly (65 years of age and over) heads of households. A separate analysis shows no bias due to the 18 percent level of non-response—at least by age, income, or race. However, not every question in the completed questionnaires was answered by every responding head of household. Because our analysis required complete information on every case, blank items reduced the number of cases available for analysis by about 20 percent. The precise extent to which this attenuation biases the results is, of course, unknown. But the strength and consistency of the observed patterns suggest that our conclusions would not be altered by complete information.

The question used to measure impatience or dissatisfaction with waiting time was contained in the Health Opinions Questionnaire and reads as follows: "Thinking over the medical care you and those close to you have received over the past few years, how satisfied have you been with waiting time in doctors' offices and clinics?" The distribution of responses to this question was dichotomized. The "very satisfied" and "satisfied" are thus distinguished from the "unsatisfied" and "very unsatisfied."

The waiting time measure, which was found in the main or general questionnaire, is formulated in the following terms: "How long do you usually have to wait to see the doctor once you get (to his office or clinic)?" This distribution was trichotomized at less than thirty minutes, thirty minutes to an hour, and an hour or more.

It will be noticed that the referent of the second question is not exactly the same as the first. The item related to satisfaction concerns the waiting time of both the respondent and those close to him, while the question that indexes waiting time itself is directed at the respondent only. However, this discrepancy is not as serious as it might appear. If a head of household is to express an opinion about the delay of another, chances are that that other is a child or some other dependent with whom the adult actually waited.

Results

The underlying hypothesis of this investigation, derived from the received theory of Catholic-Protestant differences, is that dissatisfaction with waiting time is most pronounced among Protestants. This hypothesis is tested in table 21, where controls are introduced for length of waiting time and appointment/walk-in status. The results not only discredit the hypothesis, they seem to contradict it.

If we first give our attention to the lower-right-hand corner of the table, we find that it is the Catholics, not the Protestants, who exhibit the most dissatisfaction with waiting time. Thirty-nine percent of the Protestants and 41 percent of the Catholics

TABLE 21.   Percentage Impatient by Waiting Time, Appointment Status, and Religion

Religion	Waiting Time[a]			
	Short	Moderate	Long	Total
Appointment				
Catholic	27 (197)	43 (81)	60 (70)	38 (348)
Protestant	25 (673)	38 (281)	63 (239)	36 (1193)
Total	26 (870)	39 (362)	62 (309)	36 (1541)
Walk-in				
Catholic	28 (40)	51 (37)*	74 (38)	50 (115)
Protestant	27 (170)	34 (176)	65 (238)	44 (584)
Total	27 (210)	37 (213)	66 (276)	45 (699)
Totals				
Catholic	27 (237)	46 (118)**	65 (108)	41 (463)
Protestant	26 (843)	36 (457)	64 (477)	39 (1777)
Total	26 (1080)	38 (575)	64 (585)	39 (2240)

Note: Number of cases given in parentheses.

[a]Waiting time is short when it is less than thirty minutes; moderate, between thirty and fifty-nine minutes; and long when it is sixty minutes or more.

*Difference in percentages is significant beyond the .10 level.

**Difference in percentages is significant beyond the .05 level.

express displeasure in this respect. It is true that a percentage difference of two points is not a substantial one. As we examine the column totals along the bottom of the table, however, it becomes apparent that the relationship between religion and impatience is contingent upon the length of waiting time itself. Among those subjected to a short delay, 27 percent of the Catholics and 26 percent of the Protestants give voice to dissatisfaction; for those who normally wait a long period of time, the corresponding percentages are 65 and 64—again, a difference of only one percentage point. For patients delayed an intermediate length of time, however, 46 percent of the Catholics and 36 percent of the Protestants exhibit a response denoting impatience. Here is a more significant 10 point difference.

This incidental finding suggests that the influence of religion is very much dependent upon inhibiting and facilitating situational factors. These may actually be felt in our own experience. When we await a service of some kind, we do not usually become impatient and irritated until some time has passed; and for a period (whose precise beginning and end are not ascertainable) we are not sure whether we should be angry or not. But once this phase has passed, the ambiguity disappears and our distress is keenly felt. It is the vague middle phase which is most susceptible to conditions external to delay as such; for its sentiments can find no reference in time, whereas those obtaining in the other phases are really overdetermined in this respect. For this reason the religious factor is suppressed under extreme (long or short) lengths of delay wherein all patients, regardless of religion, are most likely to feel equally pleased or distressed; but in the intermediate time interval, which is ambiguous in the sense of being neither very long nor very short, the religious factor is activated.

The above pattern maintains itself regardless of appointment status.[3] The percentage differences in dissatisfaction among walk-in patients undergoing short and long waits are one and nine, respectively—with the Catholics still displaying the most impatience; in the moderate delay category, however, the difference expands to 17 points. Among patients with *appointments*, the tendency for Catholics to be most impatient continues to be strongest under the condition of moderate delay, although this association does not appear to be as pronounced here as among walk-in patients.

The unexpectedly high level of Catholic impatience is also independent of income, as table 22 demonstrates. The specific measure used in this table is the total before-tax income of all family members, whose distribution was dichotomized at poverty level, as determined by the Bureau of Labor Statistics.[4] In a separate analysis, we found that the substitution of absolute income or education would in no way affect the conclusions drawn when the poor/non-poor dichotomy is employed.

The row totals of this tabulation show that among the non-poor a higher percentage of patients displeased with delays are Catholic (39 as opposed to 34 percent). Comparable figures for the poor are 45 and 45 percent. However, this pattern changes in some of the subgroups created by the control of waiting time, although the most pronounced differences are no longer confined to the moderate delay interval: thirteen points separate the Catholics and Protestants among both the non-poor with long delays and the poor with moderate waiting times. While these are the largest differences, it may be significant that

TABLE 22.   Percentage Impatient by Waiting Time, Poverty Level, and Religion

| Religion | Waiting Time | | | |
	Short	Moderate	Long	Total
Poor				
Catholic	31 (70)	47 (45)*	62 (48)	45 (163)
Protestant	27 (289)	34 (209)	71 (280)	45 (778)
Total	28 (359)	36 (254)	70 (328)	45 (941)
Non-Poor				
Catholic	26 (167)	45 (73)	67 (60)*	39 (300)*
Protestant	25 (557)	38 (249)	54 (198)	34 (1004)
Total	25 (724)	40 (322)	57 (258)	35 (1304)
Totals				
Catholic	27 (237)	46 (118)**	65 (108)	41 (463)
Protestant	26 (846)	36 (458)	64 (478)	39 (1782)
Total	26 (1083)	38 (576)	64 (586)	39 (2245)

*Difference in percentages is significant beyond the .10 level.
**Difference in percentages is significant beyond the .05 level.

three of the other four comparisons in the body of the table also show more impatience among Catholics.

However this may be, we are still in no position to conclude that Catholic patients tend to be more disturbed about waiting time than Protestant patients. One of the more compelling reasons for caution in this regard is the fact that Catholics tend to live in urban areas, and it is the *metropolitan* life which, according to Simmel (1950: 413), requires "the most punctual integration of all activities and mutual relations." By contrast, in the countryside and in small towns, where a sizeable proportion of the Protestants live, the pace of life is supposed to be slower, with less preoccupation with schedules, timing, appointments, and punctuality. Accordingly, the disproportionately high level of impatience among Catholics might disappear, or be reversed, if comparisons were made within and outside of metropolitan areas. Or, residence rather than religion may be the real correlate of displeasure with delay. It turns out, however, that neither possibility is borne out by the evidence.

Table 23 furnishes a breakdown of the relationship between religion and waiting time dissatisfaction by length of delay in metropolitan (city-suburban) and nonmetropolitan (town-farm) communities. Looking first to the row totals, we find that a higher level of impatience among Catholics appears to be the case within each of the two types of communities, although neither difference is very large. Turning to the body of the table, however, we find a significant relationship in the moderate delay interval for metropolitan residents, among whose Catholics a 50 percent impatience rate obtains, compared to a 37 percent rate for Protestants. In addition, three of the other five differences in the body of this table show most impatience among Catholics.

TABLE 23.   Percentage Impatient by Waiting Time, Residence, and Religion

	Waiting Time			
Religion	Short	Moderate	Long	Total
Metropolitan Communities				
Catholic	27 (192)	50 (84)*	64 (83)	42 (359)
Protestant	25 (544)	37 (253)	66 (304)	39 (1101)
Total	26 (736)	40 (337)	66 (387)	40 (1460)
Nonmetropolitan Communities				
Catholic	29 (45)	35 (34)	68 (25)	40 (104)
Protestant	26 (302)	34 (205)	69 (174)	38 (681)
Total	27 (347)	34 (239)	69 (199)	38 (785)
Totals				
Catholic	27 (237)	46 (118)*	65 (108)	41 (463)
Protestant	26 (846)	36 (458)	64 (478)	39 (1782)
Total	26 (1083)	38 (576)	64 (586)	39 (2245)

*Difference in percentages is significant beyond the .05 level.

Although the direction of the relationship between religion and impatience is not negated by residence, there are other characteristics which are very closely associated with religion and may therefore explain or reverse the effects we have up to now observed. The most important of these is race, or, rather, the subcultural time perspectives associated with it. A widely accepted assumption is that Negroes are on the whole unconcerned about time; it is said that they tend not to appear punctually for work, fail to keep appointments, and certainly do not worry if others fail to honor appointments with them. These tendencies have come together in the popular imagination in the form of the "step 'n fetch it" syndrome and have led many observers to distinguish between a "white people's time" and a "colored people's time." The fact that most Negroes are Protestants suggests that we should separate out the factor of race before analyzing Catholic-Protestant differences. Table 24 is constructed with this problem in mind.

TABLE 24.   Percentage Impatient by Waiting Time, Race, and Religion

Religion	Waiting Time			
	Short	Moderate	Long	Total
Whites				
Catholic	27 (224)	47 (110)*	63 (103)	41 (437)*
Protestant	22 (642)	34 (316)	58 (237)	32 (1195)
Total	24 (866)	34 (426)	60 (340)	35 (1632)
Blacks				
Catholic	31 (13)	25 (8)	100 (5)	42 (26)
Protestant	36 (204)	42 (142)	69 (241)	51 (587)
Total	36 (217)	41 (150)	70 (246)	50 (613)
Totals				
Catholic	27 (237)	46 (118)*	65 (108)	41 (463)
Protestant	26 (846)	36 (458)	64 (478)	39 (1782)
Total	26 (1083)	38 (576)	64 (586)	39 (2245)

*Difference in percentages is significant beyond .05 level.

Unfortunately, there are only twenty-six Negro Catholics in the entire sample. Therefore, little can be said about the inconsistent Catholic-Protestant differences among blacks. For whites, however, the pattern is steadier and sharper. Regardless of the amount of time they are usually delayed, Catholics exhibit the highest levels of displeasure. Among those who wait the least, 27 percent of the Catholics and 22 percent of the Protestants indicate impatience; in the long delay category the comparable figures are 63 and 58 percent. The association is strongest, however, in the moderately delayed group; there, 47 percent of the Catholics express impatience—13 percent more than we find among Protestants.

Incidentally, as we make note of these religious differences, we must also observe that the direction of racial differences is not what some might expect it to be. It is the blacks, not the whites, who express the most resentment over waiting time.[5]

An additional and final set of data is offered in table 25. These tabulations show the connection between religion and impatience to be invariant with respect to a number of other variables, namely, the general level of a patient's health, as well as the patient's age and sex.[6]   Though each of these variables is

TABLE 25.   Percentage Impatient by Waiting Time, Age, Sex, Health, and Religion

| Religion | Waiting Time | | | |
	Short	Moderate	Long	Total
Age: –65				
Catholic	30 (183)	55 (83)*	68 (82)	45 (348)
Protestant	30 (611)	42 (318)	66 (355)	43 (1284)
Total	30 (794)	44 (401)	67 (437)	43 (1632)
Age: 65 +				
Catholic	18 (54)	23 (35)	54 (26)	28 (115)
Protestant	13 (235)	24 (140)	57 (123)	27 (498)
Total	14 (289)	24 (175)	56 (149)	27 (613)
Male				
Catholic	29 (173)	43 (91)	67 (64)	40 (328)
Protestant	28 (564)	38 (300)	59 (265)	38 (1129)
Total	28 (737)	39 (391)	61 (329)	39 (1457)
Female				
Catholic	23 (64)	56 (27)*	61 (44)	42 (135)
Protestant	20 (282)	32 (158)	70 (213)	39 (653)
Total	21 (346)	36 (185)	68 (257)	40 (788)
Health: Good–Excellent				
Catholic	29 (188)	42 (90)	63 (68)	39 (346)
Protestant	26 (609)	36 (307)	63 (268)	37 (1184)
Total	26 (797)	38 (397)	63 (336)	37 (1530)
Health: Fair–Poor				
Catholic	22 (49)	57 (28)*	68 (40)	46 (117)
Protestant	25 (236)	35 (151)	65 (210)	42 (597)
Total	25 (285)	38 (179)	66 (250)	42 (714)

*Difference in percentages is significant beyond .05 level.

indirectly associated with religion in this sample, none of them negate its association with impatience. In each of the three tabulations an identical pattern appears: the largest and most significant differences are to be found among patients who face moderate delays and these differences are always in the direction of greater impatience among Catholics.

The only question that remains is whether the variables introduced as controls in a sequential manner might negate or reverse the direction of the religious effect if they were controlled simultaneously. The answer to this question is that they would not. In a very extensive series of separate analyses, we were unable to negate the more or less summary findings that we have presented here. As a matter of fact, the failure to do so was a source of disappointment, inasmuch as we wished to account for the results with a measured variable instead of speculative reasoning, on which we are presently forced to rely.

Conclusion

The above findings admit of at least one of two conclusions. The first is that an early Protestant attitude toward time has in the contemporary order somehow become more typical of Catholics. A second and perhaps more credible account is that while the meaning of time among Catholics and Protestants continues to differ, the former's conception produces the most impatience. Thus, while Catholics may not share the typically Protestant aversion to idleness, they may be committed to and find satisfaction in punctuality for its own sake, so that delay would cause distress regardless of whether the client had something better to do with his time. This formulation would be consistent with a higher level of impatience among Catholics. It would also conform to the consistent finding of a direct relationship between American Catholicism and "dogmatism," for the latter is centrally informed by a love of order and a rigid and narrow time perspective (Rokeach 1960). In this connection, there may be a purely symbolic element as well: unexpectedly long delays embody the very antithesis of disciplined social order and may for that reason be deplored by those for whom discipline is an absolute benefit. But this is a speculation which may presume a stronger relationship between Catholicism and dogmatism than actually obtains, and which, in any event, the present data do not allow us to verify.

However, the empirical outcomes which invite such speculation are far less ambiguous. These results show that Catholic citizens of at least one highly industrialized and predominantly Protestant nation show more regard for the typically modern concerns of punctuality and delay than the Protestant citizens of this same nation. This is to say that the relationship between religion and impatience must be determined at least in part by context: in those relatively traditional societies which have overwhelming Catholic populations, the time perspective of Catholic citizens is broad and tolerant; but in a more modern and temporally integrated bureaucratic order, the otherwise dormant elements of Catholic discipline may be activated and so shape the narrowest and strictest time perspective. Thus, a minority may actually become more attuned to an order than the majority which originally created it.

In summary, the results of this investigation show that the modern prerequisite of institutionalized punctuality is consistent with and can be satisfied by typically Catholic as well as Protestant modes of belief and cognition. This finding can only confirm the assumption that while a complex, punctually integrated industrial order may have had its origins in early Protestant thought and feeling, it seems no longer to be sustained by these ideas and sentiments alone.

8 Notes on the Social Psychology of Waiting

Waiting is painful because it causes us to renounce more productive or rewarding ways of using time. However, waiting may also be costly in itself, notwithstanding the value of foregone alternatives. This latter tendency deserves more attention than it has received. That we may detest a delay even when there is nothing else to do may strike us as an acceptable, though altogether banal, observation. Actually, it is a very extraordinary one, for if we indeed had no more attractive alternatives in mind and nothing more profitable to do with our time, having to wait would be at worst a neutral prospect rather than one that should repel us. This being so, it devolves upon us to search out the sources of distress that are immanent in waiting itself, rendering it an inferior alternative to doing nothing in some other way. This objective is important because it invites inquiry into the limits of a purely utilitarian conception of time, which, through its emphasis on waste and inefficiency, confines itself to the purely functional aspects of delay. While such a model does clarify the relationship between waiting time and its measurable costs, it fails to reckon with costs which may be nonmeasurable and irreducible.

We assume that profitable alternatives foregone through waiting are extrinsic disadvantages, as opposed to costs which are intrinsic to delay itself and independent of the value of what is disclaimed. In this essay we propose to analyze two types of intrinsic disadvantages: (1) painful psychological adjustments to delay (i.e., properties specific to "queues of one") and (2) those uniquely generated by the copresence of two or more waiters.

Some Psychological Aspects of Immobility

To wait, according to one popular dictionary, is "to stay or remain in expectation, as of an anticipated action or event"; or, "to be or remain in readiness." These definitions are references to what some psychologists would call incomplete situations or "gestalts"; in more contemporary terms, they would be defined as "unbalanced" or "dissonant" states. To all such conditions, moreover, correspond an attendant strain and a consequent tendency to restructure cognition and activity in such a way as to gain relief from it. In waiting, however, the activity that can bring about this kind of closure must be initiated by the server; the client can do little himself to achieve such a consummation: he is immobilized in a state of unfinished business.[1]

To say that waiting is an anticipatory mode simply means that it imposes constraints on attention; that is, it draws attention to time itself, which, being without inherent content, passes more slowly precisely because it is attended to. Thus, we often judge the waiting period to be longer than it is because we then pay more attention to time than we would ordinarily do during an objectively longer active period. In itself, however, this tendency is of no interest at all; it merits our attention only because it occasions so much displeasure. And yet there is no apparent reason why this should be so; indeed, just the opposite result is to be expected: if it is true that our time is finite and scarce, then just as we welcome noninflationary conditions in the monetary realm, so should we savor those circumstances which "expand" our available time. That we actually find time to be a burden is a dilemma which could only come about if an affective process interfered with its purely cognitive reckoning.

We know of no way to deal with this issue except by relying on a model of personality that, while having found its classical expression in Freud, has in a modified version informed the writings of many contemporary sociologists. We shall nevertheless confine ourselves to the basic features of this model and take care not to push them farther than we must.

As our point of departure, we propose that the experience of waiting be described in terms of an inward reallocation of involvement; that is to say, a transfer of "cathexis" from external objects to internal ones. From this displacement, typical consequences may be assumed to evolve. The most important of these is a weakening of an individual's control over otherwise repressed or, shall we say, unconscious, impulses. This is most likely to occur during periods of suspension of interaction (like waiting), when the ego, which is no longer needed for dealing with the outside world, relaxes its defenses and permits unconscious impulses to become more assertive than they would otherwise be. This is precisely what happens to us when we go to sleep or withdraw into privacy, or whenever we no longer need to censor ideas and impulses that might interfere with the successful pursuit of our goals.

But in waiting something unique occurs. Because newly assertive but still unconscious demands have by definition no consciously felt content, the ego's reestablishment of control over them (while it simultaneously liberates itself from substantive external concerns) is manifested in the feeling of boredom. Bettelheim puts this more precisely: waiting, he suggests (1965: 113), is "likely to be experienced as empty but nevertheless exhausting, and above all as boring. This feeling of unpleasantness or boredom is the overt expression of unconscious anxiety, or at least of strong tensions without any definite or conscious content." In the absence of anything constructive to do, then, waiting energy is employed in the service of repression, which, in the psychic economy, can only occur at the cost of boredom. The socially disengaged self is then free to become its own burden.

But if cessation of active contact with the external world is a source of distress, one need only reestablish a connection to gain relief. The diversions supplied in many waiting facilities, such as music or reading material, help accommodate this need. They enable a client to transfer his involvement to external objects and so forestall the activation of affective inner contents. However well-appointed, though, waiting facilities are only meant to give the waiter "*something* to do" rather than "something to *do*." Magazines, for example (which are often dated, bland, and in any case shared with other clients), are frequently only leafed through, with one eye on their pictures and another on the door leading to the server's office; the client is thereby occupied, but in a superficial and sometimes distraught way. He adopts the kind of frantic busyness characteristic of those burdened with unmanageable leisure: he seems to find himself faced with time that must be killed because it cannot be utilized. But of course this is only a metaphor. What the bored waiter has on his hands is not time at all; rather, he is burdened with the task of censoring impulses inconveniently activated by the suspension of interaction.

To engage the external world, however, is only one method of sublimation; another is fantasy. Finding their source in disengaged libidinal energy, that is to say, energy freed from external object cathexis, fantasies can be richest and most elaborate during periods in which interaction has been suspended. If this is so, then those who fantasize the most should experience the least boredom and so exhibit what would seem to be the most patience, which an experiment by Singer (1961) shows to be precisely the case. However, if fantasy alleviates boredom in a laboratory, it may create a far more serious problem in natural settings. The reason for this should soon become clear.

While boredom is symptomatic of ego's successful blocking of unconscious expression, fantasy may be symptomatic of its default: fantastic manifestations can mean that ego's repressive efforts have not been entirely effective. Accordingly, whatever strengthens ego controls in waiting subverts fantasy, and whatever weakens ego controls, like very long periods of waiting without involvement opportunities, subserves fantasy. On the other hand, the inner life is subject to distinct situational constraints; for, were individuals permitted to regress deeply into themselves, they would not be available for immediate use by the server or others (Slater 1963); they might not even be able to take advantage of service and so disrupt the organization of affairs it is meant to facilitate. While waiting for a traffic light to change, for instance, a motorist may fall so deeply into reverie as to fail to take his turn on the go signal, and so delay others. Unrestricted permission to fantasize would thus allow the waiter to withdraw cathexis from the social circles which require it and weaken his ties to these circles. And, in reference to their specifically ceremonial aspect, this sort of license would be inconsistent with the rule that people who wait take care not to gaze emptily into space or allow themselves to fall into an undignified posture, lest it appear that their concerns are not where they should be, or, perhaps, that they have no concerns at all.

Now what we have said in effect is that there is really no fully efficient way to cope with the distress of waiting. During the waiting period the individual usually finds too few materials at hand to sufficiently engross himself so as totally to prevent boredom. On the other hand, radical fantastic engrossments constitute a form of social regression, which is functionally harmful and normatively prohibited. Thus, whether the individual feels best when his ego is fully engaged or fully relaxed, waiting may be inherently bothersome because it admits of neither possibility.

Delay as Ritual Insult

If, as assumed, waiting involves an expectant attitude, it is also true that that attitude is passive, referring as it does to someone in the client's world who is actively capable of supplying a benefit or service of some kind. But this is only to say that to be in waiting is to lack direct control over desired or necessary resources. One who is in a position to cause another to wait, therefore, has power over him. Boredom is thus related to the same dependency relations which govern waiting. Or, by simple transposition, we might say that waiting may not only bore a client but subordinate him as well. On the other hand, this latter possibility has only indirectly to do with the strictly psychic costs which clients incur in having to wait; it is more a matter of resulting moral sentiment. Hence the difficulty of ascertaining the extent to which the displeasure of boredom results from its internal effects, as opposed to the sense of degradation which, in some measure or other, inevitably accompanies it.

There are at least two reasons for making this distinction. First, to render oneself motionless for the sake of another has always been one of the most humiliatingly radical forms of subordination. Indeed, in becoming inanimate by reason of dependence upon another, one might be said to descend psychologically to the category of an inanimate thing. This form, as well as its subjective expression, is quite common in social life: the ritual prostration of the devout; the rigid, military stance of attention in face of a superior; the cessation of activity as a sign of respect for the lofty—these and other modes of deferential self-suspension, though they appear to have little in common with it, find their parallel in the still expectancy of the waiter. Secondly, to be kept waiting, even in the absence of better things to do, is to be subject to an assertion that one's own time (and, therefore, one's social worth) is less valuable than the time and worth of the one who imposes the wait. Both of the above implications are confirmed by the fact that an apology ritually follows a greeting to the person whom one has immobilized and delayed. Indeed, in the absence of such implication, the apology itself would be quite unexplainable. An analysis of the apology ritual can therefore highlight the degradational dimension which is its referent.

The apology serves as a re-equilibrating mechanism in that it restores the original allotment of ritual regard that was disturbed by the delay. Thus, by enunciating the phrase, "Sorry to keep you waiting," and following with a reference to some extenuating circumstance, the latecomer announces in effect that his tardiness is unintentional and therefore "meaningless," not to be taken as an expression of his evaluation of the worth of the victim's time. The clarity of the apology is of course coordinated with the length of time that one has kept another waiting. Thus, according to Hall (1959: 16), when the offender causes another to wait beyond a certain (culturally designated) limit he is compelled to "mumble something" by way of apology when he makes his appearance; to make another wait even longer requires of the offender a clear, unambiguous apology, which would entail a full account of the delay.

The insult implied in keeping another waiting may be fore-stalled not only by measured apologizing after a delayed appearance but also by announcing beforehand that one may be late. This device, by spelling out possible extenuating circumstances before they occur, neutralizes the denial of worthiness that would otherwise be implied.

We are not surprised to find that the apology ritual tends to mediate relationships between equals more than among super-ordinates and their inferiors. Indeed, on an interactional level, the powerful are to be defined in terms of their immunity from the norms which bind their subordinates; they are exempt from the ritualistic observance by which equals defend their own dignity and protect the dignity of peers. Thus, apologies are often not provided by the doctor who keeps a patient waiting long beyond the designated appointment (least of all to a clinic patient); nor will the judge apologize to the contestants whom he has kept waiting all day (least of all to the jailed defendant). In these and in innumerably similar cases the apology ritual is not initiated because the unequal apportionment of worthiness (to which that ritual is remedially directed by an equal) is taken for granted by a superordinate. It goes without saying, moreover, that in such highly impersonal and unscheduled mass-processed queues as are found in banks and supermarkets apologies are made unnecessary by the nature of the server-client relationship itself, which, by definition, can neither take account of nor generate implications with respect to a client's social worth.

Regressive Possibilities in the Server-Client Relationship

It has been said that a sense of degradation inheres in waiting when delay implies that the client is the less worthy party in a relationship with a server. Although this statement may formulate the meaning of waiting for an objective observer, it may not fully capture its significance for the subject. Specifically, and without reference to the issue of power and exchange (see chapter 1), we may admit that a sense of inferiority may be amplified because it reanimates sentiments associated with subordinate positions the individual may have occupied in the past.

The earliest and most radical of such circumstances is infancy itself, for during this time a child is utterly dependent upon the disposition of a server (parent) for the satisfaction of many of his physical and social needs. The plain fact that the immobile infant "cannot wait" for such satisfaction—so well exemplified in his wailing demands for food—is perhaps paradigmatic (though by no means determinative) of the irritation and exasperation of the adult who must wait for the meeting of his needs. Such a parallel, though chronologically far-fetched, is sociologically compelling, for unambiguous power differences are found in both of the cases to which we refer. In both we confront a stationary and suppliant inferior incapable of satisfying his needs in any manner other than through the activity of a superior whose dominance hinges on his being uniquely able to provide for them.

A related point is that waiting itself entails regulation of a desire for service which in its earliest as well as current manifestation could only be imposed by an outside authority. In at least this connection the instillation of patience becomes a central problem of socialization. Psychoanalysts are here given to finding anal parallels, a tendency based on the idea that "awareness of the flow of time, especially the ability to measure time, unconsciously is deeply rooted in how often defecation has to take place, at which intervals it has to be done, how long the process itself should take, how long it may be successfully postponed, and so on" (Fenichel 1945: 282). There is a grain of truth in this seemingly odd proposition, in that societies which require their children to wait patiently and without complaint until they are on or by a toilet usually compel their adults to wait with similar dignity for the gratification of their particular needs. Patience with regard to the toilet therefore prefigures patience in the queue—but only insofar as both relate to a common (renunciatory) cultural pattern (see Meerloo 1966: 241–42, 249).

However, the deferred gratification pattern may be adhered to with ambivalence toward those who cause and enforce it. Just as a child may have to cope with hostility toward the ones who would deny him the pleasure of relieving himself at will, so the adult must suppress his rage at having to queue up for the serving of his immediate wants. Most of the time these feelings are satisfactorily controlled; in other instances they may not be. Just as the child may revolt against parental constraint by "holding in" what is supposed to go out at toilet time, so the adult may retaliate against his being delayed by delaying others (holding back, as it were) when he gets the chance to do so. Indeed, by keeping others (particularly superiors) waiting, some persons may experience the same satisfaction they gained by revengefully retaining their feces as children (see, for example, Adler 1916: 361–62). The anal syndrome may thus find expression in, shape, and in turn be shaped by organized power relations.

Waiting is painful because it involves deferral of gratification by an authority who is at once its source and censor. Waiting is degrading because it reawakens the social context in which these permissions and constraints were originally felt. There can be no doubt but that the central theme of this context is the irresistible authority of the parent. It must now be said that that person, besides withholding and granting material benefits to his "dependents," may himself be the object of a desire for whose satisfaction these same helpless ones must wait. This may be witnessed routinely among youngsters who wait breathlessly at the end of each workday "for daddy [often mommy] to come home." These same sentiments, we repeat, often find expression in, amplify, and reinforce the feelings generated by servers in many different queuing contexts in later life.

All of this is not to say that waiting is a regressive phenomenon but that insofar as it sociologically replicates infantile or childish helplessness it inherently admits of regressive possibilities. The precise means through which this potential may realize itself is "transference," whereby the present server becomes symbolic of what the original server was, and so may find himself to be the object of ambivalent feelings to which another is more entitled. This statement is perfectly consistent with the fact that transference does not occur randomly but is sociologically structured, activated by an individual's participation in a situation whose power distribution reproduces that in which the transferred feelings were originally and perhaps ambivalently felt. The server, then—very much like the father—may be at once despised because of the renunciations that he demands and embraced for the benefits he is capable of conferring. Accordingly, when one steps into the role of waiter he not only assumes a self but also confronts a previous self whose feelings may inform (by becoming part of) those which are evoked by current circumstances. While consciously looking forward to the forthcoming engagement, then, the waiter may be subconsciously looking backward, and subordinating himself by doing so.

Waiting As Social Interaction

One might say that our statements have up to now concerned psychological phenomena that, while they by no means presuppose him, could be readily applied to the individual waiting in isolation. However, such a summative formulation would becloud the fact that boredom, fantasy, and degradation are not solipsistic phenomena at all but rather exist in and grow out of a typical point in the unfolding of a social relationship. This qualification is an important one, for without it we might be inclined to conceive of the wait as a mere vegetative state devoid of that of which other kinds of interaction are full. Such a misconception is advanced by those who treat waiting as an intermission between "dominant involvements" and assume it to be in this sense "subordinate" to them (Goffman 1963: 44).[2] Such an observation seems to be made from an ill-advised point of view. By reifying the analytic distinction between "dominant involvements" and the "subordinate involvements" of waiting, we tend to construe action that takes place in the dominant engagement with the server as isolated from the waiting period which precedes it. Empirically, this is precisely what does not happen. Because the subjective meaning of the wait itself tempers and is in some respects affected by the kind of social relationship that immediately follows, these two parts, though temporally separate, are in fact aspects of the same whole. The waiting period precedes the engagement only in that, psychologically, it constitutes its beginning; the engagement itself is therefore one manifestation of a process that started during the wait. This is to say that waiting is itself a social relationship. Because the server can decide to make a client wait to see him, and since the client can agree to wait to be seen, each side of the relationship affects the other at a distance, with the sense in which they are separated serving merely as the definitive condition of the sense in which they are not.

The anticipation that is definitive of waiting is an intrinsic aspect of this social relationship. But as soon as we extend the connection outward in space to include other clients as well as forward in time to the server, the sociological significance of waiting becomes more complex; it then involves emergent interactional characteristics that act back upon the initial psychological state of the waiting person. We refer here to the more general problem of copresence and its effects.

As soon as a second client is added to a queue, its original constituent is subjected to something new—namely, social involvement; the second client, too, finds himself open for monitoring and interaction. This possibility suggests that the discomfort of waiting may derive not only from its association with boredom and more rewarding interactions disclaimed, but also from subjugation to the presence of those with whom the waiter is unacquainted and in whose presence he may feel uneasy.

This sense perhaps finds its most exaggerated expression in super-subordinate relationships. After all, the very existence of separate facilities, like special executive elevators or exclusive waiting rooms, presupposes superordinates' sense of being intruded upon by having to wait in the company of inferiors. Yet, theirs is but a specimen of a very widespread sentiment which leads to the segregation of the physically contaminated (such as carriers of contagious diseases in clinics and doctors' offices) and the socially contaminated (such as [formerly] Negroes in train and bus stations, and other public waiting areas). One of the sociologically most important features of the queue, then, is the way it is separated from other queues. On the other hand, social defilement in waiting is not entirely obviated by this kind of differentiation.

Symbolic and Aesthetic Aspects of Waiting

Whatever the characteristics of its members may be, contamination occasioned by co-presence is most pointed when it is structured in the form of a line. This implication may be drawn from the symbolic properties of the back, at least one of which all queuers but one must attend. It points in turn to the more general problem of face-to-back (as opposed to face-to-face) relationships as a social form and raises questions about the characteristics which are unique to it—and independent of the attending phenomenon of "crowding" and its related norms.

While the back may manifest attractive or even erotic qualities, these are opposed by a latent symbolic characteristic which sometimes overcomes them and actually repels others. To be compelled to bear witness to the back portion of another's body has long been a source of subordination and debasement in Western society. In many aristocratic settings, for instance, a subject taking leave of a royal personage must take several paces backward while still facing him and only expose his back parts by turning around after passing beyond a certain—so to speak, sacred—radius. Similarly, the practice of "turning one's back on another" is generally considered to be a form of ritual rejection whose most radical variation, perhaps, consists in the rebellious, conspicuous display or even baring of the buttocks. The symbolic inferiority of the back seems in fact to be centered in that specific region. Such connotation no doubt informs well-known verbal insults related to it and may have, on the other hand, prompted one of Freud's famous patients to surmise that the divine figure of Christ could have had no behind (1963: 251).

While it may not be possible to determine the origin of such symbolism, we may point out its affinity with popular aversion toward such forms of sexual intercourse as might entail mounting the back of another (as is typical among nonhuman animals). This disdain finds at least a terminological parallel in the often-heard objection to being made to line up too closely—to have to stand "on top of one another." The symbolic union of waiting in line and the possession of low, animallike characteristics also manifests itself in the expression, "standing in line like a bunch of cattle." This same association has been applied to Jewish victims who were "lined up like sheep" to go to the gas chamber.

If lining up in close proximity to another is a symbolic contamination, then one may be especially profaned when that other is of a lower social type. Such contingencies can and have been effectively eliminated by etiquette, which simply forbids the despised ever to place themselves in front of the worthy. In the deep South, for instance, white persons were and in some places no doubt continue to be served before black persons, regardless of order of arrival (Doyle 1937: 153). But when, in places having massive dealings with the public, that practice threatened to eliminate the Negro's patronage, separate queues and servers were provided for him (ibid.). Although by this arrangement a Negro might actually be accorded more rapid service, at least the white could never be exposed to a black back. The privilege of priority might then be said to have yielded to the taboo of face-to-back proximity.

We should recognize that the queuing experience may be aesthetically as well as symbolically displeasing. For the parts of the body to which we call attention (the back and buttocks, and rear portion of the head, neck, and legs) are precisely those whose grooming is most difficult to supervise. For this reason, the backs to which we are customarily exposed while waiting in line are likely to be rumpled, stained, or sweaty.

To have to stand in line is aesthetically noxious for another reason. The queuer, after all, is not only an object but also a *source* of contamination, which is an embarrassment that adversely acts back upon him. Being subject to exposure of another's hind-parts, he also is compelled to expose his own without opportunity to see as to their fitness for presentation. In this respect, there is some realistic basis for the typical feeling that he has lost all control over the information he wishes to convey about his body, that he is being closely watched and, worst of all, possibly evaluated with disgust by the person behind him. This paranoic sense, more common than might be initially supposed, manifests itself in popular idiom: "Get off my back" and "Don't breathe down my neck"—as well as the classic desire to "sit with one's back to the wall." These expressions could hardly admit of such general use did they not embody an equally widespread anxiety about those positioned behind. This queer feeling is understandable in terms of the considerations we have enumerated. While we may control those before us by exerting control over how we appear to them—and even assess (by assessment of their reactions) the way we appear in their imagination—we know not what impression we make on those behind us, nor what they think about that impression. It is of course true that the "norm of inattention" sometimes protects us in this regard from the prying glances of others; but the very existence of that norm presupposes that there may be something nasty about us that deserves the attention of others. Thus, a protective rule which causes others to purposely avoid us (in the visual sense, at least) could only confirm the existence of something to be ignored.

The above statements will of course be rejected by those who fail to experience the sentiments just described. And yet these will be the first to admit that, when in line, they are not unaware of the body in front of them and as a matter of fact are prevented only by civility from scrutinizing it at great length. It is as if there existed a structured pattern of ignorance whereby each person violates another's reserve (in a disciplined way, to be sure) but assumes himself immune—a tendency which, incidentally, can only reduce the pain of the social necessity of lining up. But this is a precarious kind of ignorance, for the person who has never given a second thought to waiting in line becomes highly sensitive and uncomfortably self-conscious as soon as he is given reasons why he should feel so, or exposed to claims that he might. This could only mean that awaiting us in lined queues are sentiments which are always available for conscious feeling, if not always consciously felt.

If no other social constraints were operating, then by reason of the aesthetic and symbolic considerations described, persons in line would tend to place between themselves a space which embodies a synthesis of two contradictory tendencies: the first consists of the individual's desire to maintain a respectable distance from other queuers. By avoiding profane contact he retains some measure of the diminished dignity which exposure to another's behind symbolizes; thereby, he also spares himself such aesthetic contamination as we have tried to describe. This is consistent with the fact that in most lines inter-queuer distance is greater at the tail-end than in the middle, just as if persons were reluctant to approach those in front of them of their own accord but only do so when the presence of another person or persons behind propels them forward.[3] It remains to be seen whether distance from the person in front is most pronounced among those who by reason of being shorter have their entire prospect dominated by the preceding person's back, as opposed to those who are taller and can disattend it. At any rate, distancing measures such as these are always opposed by a desire not to give offense by standing beyond a "sociable" distance, for to do so would deny the worthiness of another to be physically approached and so constitute an affront. Of course, the purely instrumental factor which militates against the maximization of inter-queuer distance to infinity is the need to mark out and protect one's priority in line.

The distancing phenomenon is notable in its qualitative as well as purely quantitative aspects. If the symbolic and aesthetic features of queuing were in fact as repulsive as has been suggested, we would expect them to find observable expression in the structure of the line itself. Persons in line would then not be expected to position themselves face forward and directly behind another but to rather tend to stand perpendicularly with respect to those in front and behind them or, at the very least, to so turn their heads in order to avoid visual contamination by the person in front while simultaneously exercising peripheral surveillance on the monitoring activity of the person in back. These expectations are confirmed by common experience. That from a distant standpoint members of a queue appear to be totally unmindful of one another is indeed one of its most conspicuous empirical features. It is as if the contaminating closeness of people in line was offset by its ritual denial, so that the external appearance of blasé indifference merely confirmed an obtusely disturbed inner state, whose absence would render that appearance functionally superfluous.

The symbolism of priority. What is said above may be distinguished and abstracted from another symbolic indignity connected with the queue. Priority, as is known, has traditionally served as a metaphor for descriptions of authority and power relationships, in that the socially superior are titularly or informally "first," while their inferiors are "last," which is to say that the former are "ahead of" or "before" those who are "behind" and "after." In this same sense, the "advanced" are better off than the "retarded," and so forth. This metaphorical connection is no doubt anchored in empirical reality, where the resourceful and prestigious enjoy factual priority over the less worthy in the satisfaction of their needs. The symbolic realm, however, can act back and transform the reality which it represents, so that the very fact of being "last," "behind," "after," or "retarded" gives rise to a real sense of inferiority that was initially only metaphorical. (This would at least justify the suspicion that the esteem of those whose family names begin with letters situated at the end of the alphabet must suffer because of it, spending as they do a lifetime—in schools, the military, business, etc.—being last.) But perhaps the degradational symbolism of inferior priority achieves its most unambiguous expression in popular anatomical reference, in that to be positioned behind another is to be exposed to his behind, which is customarily described in pejorative terms such that an axis of profane contact may be envisioned at whose degenerate pole we find diverse modes of bodily contact between the front of one and back parts of another. But this is a matter of deviance in face-to-back relationships, which is beyond our intended realm.

Conclusion

The purpose of this chapter was to outline some of the senses in which waiting is distressful independently of the aspect of involuntarily renounced alternatives. Such displeasure was shown to inhere exclusively in waiting, which is one particular form of doing nothing, without reference to idleness itself (against which, in the West, at least, there are culturally grounded warnings). It is always possible, of course, to suggest that the psychological and symbolic disadvantages of waiting are themselves costs and may therefore be assimilated to those involved in the forfeiture of alternative rewards. But this would be to place on a single plane facts of entirely different orders. The boundary between these realms seems to emerge when we recognize that more profitable alternatives foregone through waiting are *extrinsic* disadvantages, as opposed to displeasures, such as those herein described, which are *intrinsically* costly, regardless of the value of what is disclaimed.[4] The two parts of this analytic distinction converge in the empirical instance: waiting is at once disadvantageous because of immanent costs unique to it and because it is instrumental to the accrual of costs outside of and having nothing to do with waiting as such. Thus, if extrinsic considerations furnish no reason for staying in a waiting room or queue, then intrinsic ones would surely cause us to leave. This follows logically, but not empirically.

Though one does join a queue for the purpose of achieving valued ends which are extrinsic to waiting, these values account only for the desire to wait in the first place; once one has decided to do so, the decision to continue is reinforced by a principle which differs from that which gave rise to the initial decision. This is evidenced among those who, after joining a queue, feel oppressed by it or decide that it is moving too slowly and conclude that further waiting would not be bearable or worthwhile. Having arrived at this decision, people may yet find it difficult to renege. What binds them to their position is a consideration that lends to waiting greater disadvantages, both intrinsic and extrinsic, than it would otherwise have. The reason is that by joining a queue the client implicitly claims sufficient command of his needs as to be capable of behaving civilly until they are met. In this he of course does no more than affirm his willingness to be the same kind of person that others who are waiting have themselves agreed to be. The impulse impatiently to abandon the queue is thus tempered by the client's assessment of others' assessments of himself; he is bound to it by a commitment to them, from which he cannot easily withdraw. The client stays because of a reluctance to define himself as the one person who "cannot wait his turn like everyone else."[5]

From this we can only conclude that people who line up for exclusively instrumental reasons must be subject to constraints which emerge out of the lining up itself, as if a purely rational economic impulse, collectively expressed, gives rise to an irrational normative reality that supercedes and negates it. A client is then bound to endure the intrinsic displeasure of waiting even when the extrinsic rationale for doing so no longer obtains.[6] It is in this sense that "patience," whose Latin root means *suffering*, is so fully apt and justified as a description of what the waiting person typically feels to be his irreducible burden, and, therefore, his only practicable option. But the norm which demands acceptance of this burden would be unnecessary if it were not at least indirectly instrumental to something beyond itself. Because its referent is our irrational loyalty to queues, that unknown must symbolize a commitment to public order, which, though that order does not require it, is nevertheless affirmed when an act of commitment is expressed as an end in itself.

4   Social Functions of Waiting

9 Some Unappreciated Consequences of Delay

In certain seemingly insignificant traits, which lie upon the surface of life, the same psychic currents characteristically unite. Modern mind has become more and more calculating. The calculative exactness of practical life which the money economy has brought about corresponds to the ideal of natural science: to transform the world into an arithmetic problem, to fix every part of the world by mathematical formulas. Only money economy has filled the days of so many people with weighing, calculating, with numerical determinations, with a reduction of qualitative values to quantitative ones.

. . . . .

Punctuality, calculability, exactness are forced upon life by the complexity and extension of metropolitan existence and are not only most intimately connected with its money economy and intellectualist character. These traits must also color the contents of life and favor the exclusion of those irrational, instinctive sovereign traits and impulses which aim at determining the mode of life from within, instead of receiving the general and precisely schematized form of life from without.

Georg Simmel, "The Metropolis and Mental Life"

If there is one assumption that pervades all of the preceding inquiries, it is that waiting can only be a negative contingency. For the client, delay means boredom, renunciation of better uses of time, and sometimes even humiliation; for the collectivity, it occasions congestion and inefficiency. But this impression comes from our having treated the subject from a limited number of standpoints; our inquiries and discussion would therefore be incomplete if we failed to show how waiting adds to our satisfaction and how it is essential to a social order which few of us would deny.

It is true that, in conjunction with money, the rigid scheduling of activities expresses the profoundest subjective level of modern urban life, with its accentuated contours of "punctuality, calculability, exactness." But while an appreciation of the schedule enriches our ideal image of the metropolis, schedular default is perhaps more characteristic of its actuality. The highly complex timetable, with the myriad and ramified interactions that it programs and symbolizes, may be celebrated in theory, but the practical life to which this theory attends seems to be constantly preoccupied with its breakdown. Associated with this is a counterimage of the metropolis, resonating not only punctuality but also a background of impersonal and uncaring irregularity: not calculability and exactness, but only an irritatingly imperfect tendency in these directions. The so-called "bustle" of the city, in this view, takes on the tone of a confused regularity rather than the Simmelian ideal of a precisely ordered busyness. This nuance bespeaks an accommodation between two seemingly irreconcilable imperatives.

The differentiated activities of the modern city are routinely synchronized only if a high value is placed on *punctuality*; but insofar as specialized services for a massive market create queuing and congestion, the opposite value of *patience* becomes a prerequisite for organized relationships. Not only a deeply installed respect for promptness, then (see Simmel 1950b: 42–413), but also a tolerance and orderly accommodation of its default make metropolitan life as efficient as it is. From this juxtaposition an ironic relationship obtains. While excessive congestion may immobilize a system and impede the achievement of its objectives, some measure of waiting facilitates the social process by enabling the system to accommodate fluctuations in server supply and client demand, as well as other extenuating circumstances, without subverting its orderly operation. In every collective enterprise, then, a foreground of specialized activity must be subserved by an equally important background of organized inactivity.

These reasons justify the conviction that orderly queuing is a prerequisite for the achievement of individual and collective ends. Moreover, because the efficient fitting together of lines of goal-directed action presumes efficiency in the organization of inaction, there is really no functional alternative to the queue. In this respect it is quite beside the point whether waiting is occasioned rationally or not, whether it is suffered more by some persons than by others, or whether temporal access to all or certain services is relatively open or restricted. These considerations have no bearing on the necessity of waiting as such. For even in the face of immediate individual costs, something must contain, on occasions when it would be systemically disadvantageous to renege from or break into a queue, those who would otherwise do so. This inhibition could only come about if the value of patience somehow developed and sustained a patient attitude that could never be realized in its absence. So far as they subordinate the substantive, idiosyncratic, or momentary meaning of waiting to its functional significance, these considerations extend it beyond mere means within a social relationship and justify waiting as an end in itself.

Delay as an Autonomous Form

While authority (at least in the Durkheimian sense) finds its most characteristic function in the closing off or regulation of opportunities for gratification, waiting definitively entails submission to such an imperative, in the form of self-imposed restraint or inhibition of desire. This being so, waiting must embody the very principle of discipline. Even more, waiting may constitute the earliest modality in which discipline is experienced.

Insofar as it regulates consummatory expression, waiting is an "ego function." The instincts say, "Now!"; the ego says, "Wait!" The ego thus becomes a "service mechanism" capable of delaying impulse. However, the capacity for self-control can be maintained only if its necessity periodically re-presents itself; in this sense, waiting is "needed" because it helps to maintain self-regulatory controls in good working order. Indeed, because it so well embodies the ends of discipline, waiting may be deliberately imposed with a view to its inculcation and reinforcement. Bettelheim (1965: 118) made this same point when he said: "If our wish is to strengthen the ego, we must give the child ample chance to exercise it . . . . While the 'in-between times' [of which waiting is an instance] often tax the child's ego strength severely, they are times which can be used very constructively in developing his ego strength." The autonomization of waiting is common in adult socialization as well. This is particularly true in authoritarian settings. In military training, for example, recruits are often called upon to move from one physical location to another with maximum speed, then wait for a very long time to engage in the business to which they so hastily brought themselves. Such a routine is embodied in the expression, "Hurry up and wait," whose practice inculcates respect for disciplined punctuality as such, independently of its instrumental value. Instances such as this would be unexplainable if waiting were not in itself a source of utility, if it did not embody the discipline which preconditions social life in its broader aspects. It can be no coincidence, then, that those who ignore this discipline are defined as having "gotten out of line."

Aesthetic aspects of autonomization. It remains to be said—though only in an incidental way—that just as waiting may constitute its own purpose, so may the form in which waiters frequently organize themselves. Often being linear, this structure has functional advantages in facilitating allocation of service; however, it also possesses high aesthetic attraction, for its containment of individual units within a designated place, whose meaning to the system-as-a-whole is located within a central (priority) principle, conveys a clear sense of symmetrical internal organization. Thus, while the act of lining up may be aesthetically repugnant to participants, the opposite impression may be found among those who witness the formation from a distant standpoint. Indeed, the aesthetic charm of the well-disciplined line, irrespective of its practical value, may be sufficient to justify its existence. This tendency is expressed most conspicuously in the daily activities of highly disciplined organizations (like educational, military, and penal institutions) whose members are periodically commanded to "line up," often for no purpose which visibly transcends the line itself. Even nursery schools cause children to move into and out of a building—or from building to playground and back—in a line. Only in part is the motive for such practices found in the usefulness of bringing order to an unorganized collectivity, or even of ritually exercising social discipline. For, while the super-ordinate may at once exercise and celebrate his authority by compelling subordinates to submit themselves to the socio-logically derogatory principle of the line, acts of power require sufficiently elegant outcomes to befit that which they sym-bolize. The line itself approximates that form, and so constitutes an object of study from the standpoint of the aesthetics as well as the sociology of power.

Delay as a Role-Transition Mechanism

Waiting promotes order (1) as a disciplined compensatory form, made necessary by the initial fact of congestion, and (2) as a ritual which indirectly promotes self-control in spheres outside of waiting itself. We now face the question of whether waiting is also demanded by principles actually immanent in the engage-ment which is its object. In assuming this to be the case, we are obliged not only to identify properties of the engagement that occasion the necessity of waiting but also to specify how the meeting of such necessity subserves the social process, in a manner above and beyond that already indicated.

Because they are required to invest so much of themselves in their dealings with others, individuals may find it difficult to disattach themselves subjectively once those dealings are objectively terminated. As a result the individual may bring into the current engagement residues (e.g., fatigue, irritation, and cognitive preoccupation) of previous ones—a tendency which finds expression in the feeling of being "rushed," "harried," or "pressed for time" (see also Fenichel [1945: 204] on "time claustrophobia"). The interactional referent of such feeling is the inability to sustain an appropriate identity in entering a new role. Here is a "system problem" in reference to which the waiting period serves an important function—for both sides of the server-client relationship.

If waiting were not inherent in those unpredictable contin-gencies which are central to the nature of modern life, some functional equivalent for it would have to be devised and institutionalized. For, without frequent delays, our daily affairs would require continual interaction, with no remission save that of physical movement from one situation to the next. The undesirability of such a state is easily confirmed. When, for example, few waiting periods are imposed by circumstances or by an outside authority, they may be effected by the individual himself, who purposely arrives early and extends his waiting time so as not to involve himself further in what he is doing without rest. Thus, a tired motorist may accelerate toward a red light in order to take voluntary advantage of the delay that it compels. Similarly, a person may appear early for an appointment and wait so as to be sure he will not be called upon to account for himself before having a chance to "pull himself together." These considerations provide an additional reason why, despite the importance of the value of punctuality in our society, a substantial measure of lateness may under some circumstances be welcomed as well as tolerated. It bears emphasizing that such willing forbearance inheres in the server-client relationship itself and not in any one of its parts. Just as a server's lateness may (up to a point) be agreeable to those who wait for him, clients' lateness may for the very same reasons be welcomed by the server. The waiting period in this way enables the server to make ready for the client in a way that often complements the client's making ready for him.

This leads to a point which may now be stated in more formal terms. Because personal engagements require some physical and/or mental preparation, an individual cannot be absorbed by them unless they are preceded by what we have elsewhere (Schwartz 1970: 488–90) called an "institutionalized transition phase," of which the waiting period is an example. This period, to summarize, is definable in terms of the functions it performs, namely, engagement *recovery* and engagement *preparation*. It can be said, then, that the waiting period (provided its length does not exceed certain limits) serves the same function in respect of *role* shifts that anticipatory socialization does with reference to *status* shifts. Whereas the latter mechanism eases passage from one status to another in movement across the life cycle, the former facilitates the passage from one role to another during movement through the daily activity cycle.

The waiting period, then, is not merely a residual phase—a quantum of time representing default in the coordination of the end of one activity with the beginning of another; rather this phase contains its own functional justification, which is to articulate social relationships, in the sense indicated. Waiting periods thus represent part of the connective tissue by which interactions are held together and ordered, according to the principle that the temporal separation of engagements constitutes the very condition of their inner coherence.

Waiting and Autonomy

The social benefits of waiting are expressed in yet another way. When we push ourselves beyond the mere observation of people waiting for and, later, interacting with one another, we infer individual decisions to begin and end a previous activity a little early or late, to pursue it at a more or less rapid pace, and to enter the current, observable engagement with varying dispatch. The malintegration of relationships (which finds expression in waiting) therefore presupposes some measure of autonomy of action and choice on the part of those engaged in them. This means that the abolition of delays in any system of human action could be brought about only at the expense of self-regulation. It would entail minute control over the activities of both clients and servers. Such an order is depicted by the Russian novelist Zamiatin (1952: 13, 97) in his antiutopian *We*. In these pages we find the most radical image of the Simmelian metropolis, wherein activities are precisely integrated by "the Tables," a modern generalization of "that greatest of all monuments of ancient literature, the "Official Railroad Guide":

> The Tables transformed each of us, actually, into a six-wheeled steel hero of a great poem. Every morning, with six-wheeled precision, at the same hour, at the same minute, we wake up, millions of us at once. At the very same hour, millions like one, we begin our work, and millions like one, we finish it. United into a single body with a million hands, at the very same second, designated by the Tables, we carry the spoons to our mouths. . . . fifty is the number of chewing movements required by the law of the State for every piece of food . . . ; at the same second we all go out to walk, go to the auditorium, to the halls for the Taylor exercises, and then to bed.

Not even the most unyielding totalitarian order could approximate the encompassing controls depicted here. What the Zamiatinian vision does convey, however, is the idea that default of synchronization presupposes some measure of autonomy of individual choice and action. Freedom makes waiting inevitable, and no authority could possibly exercise the total controls that would be necessary to do away with it (notwithstanding the famous dictator's success in finally getting Italian trains to run on time).

Inasmuch as tolerance of delay subserves the unwillingness of members of a social system to be too rigidly bound by the norm of punctuality, they are enabled, at the expense of those who wait for them, to enter into an engagement a little late in order to indulge mood, disposition, extenuating circumstances, and the like. By thus safeguarding the very conditions that make it necessary, the waiting period reinforces the boundary within which individuals are free to supervise their own economies of action. Accordingly, an institutionalized willingness to wait is not only expressive of a collective resignation to abide some organizational flaw which denies to individuals their desire for immediate access to others; it also works in a more positive way by enabling the organization to accommodate some degree of autonomy on the part of its members—along with the schedular inefficiency that such freedom entails—without subverting its orderly operation. On the other hand, tolerance of delay may enhance rather than detract from efficiency when the object of autonomy is efficiency itself, in that a server may delay a client for the sake of highly important business whose completion would be systemically advantageous. A measure of permissiveness with respect to delay thus leads to the flexibility of an organization as well as the autonomy of its members. So when we take a sufficiently comprehensive (i.e., macroscopic) point of view, the manifestly negative aspects of waiting and congestion appear to serve quite positive ends.

The question still remains as to whether the *individual* gains of waiting tend generally to cancel out the losses over time and whether, at a given point in time, net gains or losses are equally or unequally distributed throughout the social structure. At each of the various points in this structure, then, we may balance off what is gained in waiting by what is lost because of it. In so doing, we may identify the individuals who incur the cost of collective autonomy and flexibility. This is largely a matter of shifting to a microanalytic level of analysis and treating waiting as an exchange relationship. But now we have come full circle and so may bring our discussion to an end.

Notes

Introduction

1. The relationship between economic growth and time scarcity is described in detail by Linder (1970) in his *Harried Leisure Class*, to which these introductory remarks are very much indebted. I have also been informed by Daniel Bell's short but very convincing argument (1973, pp. 456–75) on the same subject. A more formal variation on this theme is to be found in economist Gary Becker's "A Theory of the Allocation of Time" (1965).

Chapter 1

1. Others wait with no possibility of being served. For a very convincing explanation of this practice, see Mann and Taylor (1969).

2. There are exceptions, however. Thus, "on some airlines, when there is a flight delay, the passengers . . . may get a meal, a long-distance call or even an overnight hotel room, all free of charge." But "with few exceptions, the availability of complimentary services is left to the initiative of those passengers who are knowledgeable enough to request them. . . . Passengers who are bashful or unaware of their rights may get nothing. . . . The Civil Aeronautics Board said four airlines indicated they will take the initiative in informing the passenger of such services. All other carriers will provide information as to services only upon the passenger's request" (*Chicago Daily News*, September 2–3, 1972: 27). The same is true with regard to the practice of "bumping." On some flights, airlines will sell more tickets than there are seats, expecting a certain percentage of those with reservations not to show up. If all do appear, the last ones to have made reservations are rejected and made to wait for the next flight. The CAB regulations entitle those so delayed to immediate compensation in the form of a fine equal to the price of the ticket (within a $25–$200 limit). Until recently, this right was honored only at the passenger's request (*Chicago Daily News*, October 10, 1972: 28).

3. Personal communication from Florence Levinsohn.

4. Other "contacts" include the radio, over which Saturday and Sunday morning waiting times at many metropolitan golf courses are broadcast. This service, which saves many players many long delays, is performed almost exclusively for the middle and upper-middle classes.

5. Even when circumstances make it necessary for the resourceful to wait, they suffer less than their inferiors. As a general rule, the wealthier the clientele,

the more adequate the waiting accommodations. Thus, persons who can afford bail can await their trial (or, far more frequently, their attorneys' bargaining on their behalf) in the free community. The poor must wait in jail. The same is true of facilities. In airports, for example, those who can afford it may simultaneously avoid contamination by the masses and engross themselves in a variety of desirable activities in "VIP lounges." The term "lounge" instead of the vulgar "waiting area" or "gate" is also applied to facilities set aside for those who travel a specified number of miles with (and pay a substantial sum of money to) a particular airline. In this as in many other settings, waiting locales for the poor and the less wealthy lack the elaborate involvement supplies, pleasant decor, and other physical and psychological comforts that diminish the pain of waiting among those who are better off.

6. A functional equivalent is found in the Soviet Union. "Aleksandr Y. Kabalkin and Vadim M. Khinchuk . . . describe what they termed 'classic cases' in everyday life in the Soviet Union, in which customers wait for the television repairman or for a messenger delivering a train or plane ticket that had been ordered by phone. To the question 'About what time can I expect you?' the stereotyped reply is, 'It can be any time during the day.' And people have to excuse themselves from work and wait—there is no other way out" (New York Times, November 7, 1971: 5).

7. It may not be assumed that all lawyers earn while they wait. For example, the New York Times (August 25, 1971: 24) recently reported: "A lawyer who specializes in prosecuting landlords' claims against tenants asked permission in Bronx Supreme Court yesterday to bring his cases there rather than in Civil Court because . . . he spent much time 'just sitting and waiting.' And consequently, he said, he was suffering 'financial loss' and felt he could not continue working in Civil Court."

8. This is to say that, as a scarce commodity, time or priority of service routinely becomes the object of struggle. Recognizing this, a court intake officer writes in a memo to his supervisor: "Intake counselors should assume more control over the setting of cases on the docket, with a proportionate decrease in the control now exercised by clerks" (Fairfax County [Virginia] Juvenile and Domestic Relations Court, Memorandum, 1971: 1).

9. Of course, the impulse of stationary servers to make others wait for reasons that are independent of the scarcity of time is paralleled by the tactic, used by mobile servers, of keeping them waiting for these same reasons. Thus, a person may simultaneously exhibit contempt for a gathering and underscore his own presence (Parkinson 1962: 73–74) by purposely arriving late. This measure is particularly effective when the proceedings require his presence.

10. This practice was explained to me by Donald N. Levine.

11. What has been said in reference to delay may also apply when clients are seen immediately. In this case, too, it is often difficult to tell whether a server wishes to ritually acknowledge a client's worth or whether that client is seen at once because there are no other demands on the server's time.

12. The subsumption of the server-client relationship under the concept of differential commitment was suggested to me by Philip Blumstein.

Chapter 2

1. In the present data the probability of a patient leaving an emergency department waiting room without treatment is directly related to that department's mean waiting time.

2. Personal communication from Dr. Peter Rosen, Director, Billings Hospital Emergency Department, University of Chicago.

3. We dichotomized at 15 minutes because it is a conventional partition of the hour. Elsewhere, we dichotomized as close to the median as possible. Because in some cases the middle category of a distribution was very large, the number of cases in the two parts of the dichotomy is not the same.

4. For example, the mean "medical urgency rating" for patients in emergency departments with less than forty daily arrivals is 2.33, as opposed to 2.27 in departments with forty or more arrivals. About 37 percent of the patients in both groups of facilities are black.

5. The five tables in this chapter admit of over 100 comparisons. Because we can find no place for them in an uncluttered text, significance levels have not been furnished. Our assumption about the stability of these results rests in any case on the consistency of the patterns they exhibit rather than the statistical significance of isolated associations.

6. Because emergency rooms with the largest number of patients and staff tend also to be those with the most equipment and facilities, they exhibit the longer diagnostic service times. Nondiagnostic "treatment time" is also longer in these departments, probably because this measure contains unknown amounts of patient delay between diagnosis and post-diagnostic treatment. There is no reason to assume that the treatment of a specific ailment would actually take longer in the larger departments. That both nondiagnostic as well as diagnostic service time is unrelated to waiting time tends to confirm this belief.

7. Among departments with low numbers of daily arrivals 9 percent of the small staffs are associated with highly differentiated facilities, as opposed to 61 percent of large staffs. The comparable percentages among high arrival departments are 33 and 71.

8. Among departments with small staffs, 22 percent of those with a low level of spatial differentiation had a high number of arrivals, as opposed to 60 percent of those with high differentiation. The quantities for the least and most differentiated units with large staffs are 58 and 68 percent. The association between space and volume, controlling for staff size, is therefore slightly higher than the relationship between staffing and patient demand, controlling for the division of space.

Chapter 3

1. Individual (as opposed to grouped) rankings were employed. Higher ranks are assigned to the higher grade departments. However, scores could be obtained for only 76 of the 176 authors whose papers were read by referees. Of the 289 referees who read and returned papers, departmental ranks are available for 168.

2. This datum was obtained from the 1970 American Sociological Association membership directory. Highest status is assigned to professors; lowest, to instructors. Author information was obtained for 121 of the 176 refereed papers. Information was available for 230 referees.

3. These data were obtained from the 1970 American Sociological Association membership directory. Information was available for 98 authors and 204 referees.

4. This datum appears in the journal's "Annual Report to the Editors and Advisory Board and Reviewers, 1973" (p. 2). No specific figure is given.

5. Personal communication from Dr. Peter Rosen, Director, Billings Hospital Emergency Department.

6. In operations research a distinction is sometimes made between "preemptive" and "head of the queue" priorities, the former referring to contingencies which cause a server to interrupt treatment of one client in favor of another; the latter to priorities which only grant a status of "next on the list." Our less precise use covers both types of preemptions.

7. Information on number of pages was available for 121 of 176 refereed manuscripts.

8. The correlations are based on 168, 230, and 204 cases respectively.

9. Correlations in the referee data are slightly distorted by the fact that some referees (whose number is unknown but probably quite small) read two or more papers. However, the significant correlations are high enough, and the insignificant correlations, low enough, to suggest that such a distortion would not affect the conclusions drawn.

10. This tendency is probably subject to seasonal variation in manuscripts received, which reach their peak during the spring and summer. The number of manuscripts returned to authors attain their peak during the fall and winter. There is an inverse relationship, by season, between number of manuscripts received and number returned. It follows that contributors who remit their papers during the spring wait the longest for their return (22.8 weeks); fall contributors have the shortest wait (14.8 weeks). Those who send in papers during the winter and summer are intermediate in this respect with a wait of about 16 weeks. This pattern maintains itself over time and within phases 2 and 3. There is no seasonal variation in manuscript queuing time in phase 1.

11. The recent appointment of a new editor to the *American Journal of Sociology* will no doubt bring with it changes in these constants, as well as an occasion to gauge their effects.

Chapter 4

1. A more gross conception of waiting can be extended to other contents, for queues form along all routes of access to a server. Accordingly, there are as many "queue modalities" as there are kinds of communication. Up to now we have referred only to clients waiting for personal engagement with servers, a formation here designated as a *primary* modality. However, clients may also gain access to servers by means of aural and written communication. Those who bid for access in these ways may also have to wait until a server is willing or able to grant attention. A phone call to an executive, for example, may

produce a busy signal or a secretarial request to wait. Likewise, a memo, report or letter may remain for some time in his "incoming" tray (waiting channel) unopened, unstudied, or unanswered. In addition to the primary kind, then, we must also recognize that a server may administer to *secondary* (telephone and correspondence) queues. We could even go further and conceive of all the day's chores as constituents of a queue, but to do so would stretch our discussion beyond the boundaries of the service system framework. In confining ourselves to its convenient limits we therefore dwell exclusively upon queuing of the primary kind.

2. Because service in order of arrival is a right rather than a duty of clients, Goffman (1971: 36) defines the dominance ranking it governs as a "positive" as opposed to a "negative" queue. Constituents of the latter are ordered with a view to being administered something they do *not* want. Another exception to the normal priority principle is the rule "first in, last out," which governs many forms of exiting behavior in public conveyances (e.g., elevators, buses, airplanes, etc.)

3. Homans's (1961: 75) formulation of the rule of distributive justice reads as follows: "A man in an exchange relation with another will expect that the rewards of each man be proportionate to his costs—the greater the rewards, the greater the costs—and that the net rewards, or profits, of each man be proportional to his investments—the greater the investments, the greater the profit." Accordingly, "The more to a man's disadvantage the rule of distributive justice fails of realization, the more likely he is to display the emotional behavior we call anger."

4. For a dramaturgical definition of scene creation, see Goffman (1959: 210).

5. Whereas the requirement that rewards be commensurate with *investments* resonates affinity with the capitalistic standard, the demand that rewards be coordinated with *needs* may be identified with the socialist criterion of justice. The Marxian formulation of distributive justice ("From each according to his abilities; to each according to his needs") thus differs in its allocational implications from Homans's counterpart.

6. In "negative queues," whose members await a dreaded service, preemptive criteria admit of claims to postponement rather than priority.

7. A combination of these models is reported from the Soviet Union by Levine (1959: 338–39):

> There is a unique Soviet system in forming lines, a queue etiquette. When word gets around that a store has received a stock of an item in short supply that will go on sale the following morning, knots of people begin to gather. However, because the police will not tolerate lines forming overnight, a sort of line "pool" is sometimes organized. Instead of people remaining in front of the store all night, a system of shoppers' guard duty is set up. By drawing lots, one person is assigned to "stand guard" at the store for each hour of the night. The names of would-be shoppers are written on a list in the order in which they arrived at the scene. Each succeeding shopping sentry is entrusted with the list that has been compiled and he, in turn, passes it on to the person who relieves him on duty. The custodian of the list enters the names of others who subsequently come to the store, having heard late of the sale, or with the intention of being the first in line. As the store's opening

approaches, crowds of shoppers arrive, names are called out, and the line forms in a more or less orderly fashion, according to the list.

8. If (disregarding exogenous sources of disturbance) lines admit of inherent stability, it follows that lines may be formed with a view to *creating* order. Lohman (1957: 145) provides an illustration:

A relief agency had sent out notices that it would employ men at a certain hour at Humboldt Park field house. When an officer arrived on the scene, a crowd of several thousand had gathered in front of the field house. The officer was confronted with a sea of heads milling about the doors. Excitement was rising, men pushed against one another, and there was danger that a protecting rail would collapse from the weight of the pressure against it. If left to its own devices, the crowd would have broken the railing, with resultant injuries, and might have stormed the building. The officer took a position where he could command the attention of the crowd and told them that if they would form an orderly line, they would all be registered in due course. He selected four men as the first elements in a column and began to march them in zigzag fashion around and away from the field house. Soon he had the whole crowd arranged in a column of fours stretched around and away from the field house.

9. Note the rules of "Ladies first," "Age before beauty," etc.
10. For an instructive demonstration, see Mintz (1951). The game theoretical standpoint is usefully brought to bear on this subject by Roger Brown (1965: 737–43). For an alternative but altogether too general point of view, see Smelser (1962: 131–69).
11. The English pattern extends beyond England itself, encompassing at least one of its former colonies, Hong Kong. William Parish, an expert on China, has in a personal communication contrasted the orderliness of queues in Hong Kong with the relatively unregulated service systems of Taipei, Formosa—a city which has never been exposed to the English mode.

Chapter 5

1. A "service system" consists of one or more "service facilities," each manned by a server or servers, and one or more "waiting channels," whose occupants constitute a queue.
2. Missing information on medical urgency was not equally distributed among emergency departments. In the busiest facilities, the investigators found it especially difficult to follow all clients through treatment and obtain medical ratings. The percentage of missing data for the smallest, middle three, and largest groups of emergency rooms are, respectively, 9.6, 7.7, 9.3, 17.4, and 21.8. Coverage for all other variables is within one percentage point of completion.
3. The correlation between an independent and dependent variable can never exceed the square root of the reliability of the independent variable.
4. There is good reason to believe that within a certain range of disorders, blacks will be assigned a lower level of acuteness than whites expressing the

same complaint. (For evidence, see Roth 1972.) This fact could only further reduce the validity of the medical urgency index. However, this problem is not of direct importance to us. In this investigation we are concerned with the manner in which the perception of urgency affects waiting time, not·with the accuracy of this perception.

5. The aggregate figure, however, is much higher. If the temporal cost of being black is 3.16 minutes per person, then the daily cost for all 1,105 blacks in the sample is 3,493 minutes, or 58 hours. The monthly cost comes to 1,746 hours; the yearly figure is almost 21,000 hours, or the equivalent of a working day for 2,619 men. This is not to mention the relatively short waiting time in Cook County emergency rooms as compared with units in other regions of the country, many of which may discriminate far more against the black patient.

6. Repeated observations at a given interval of time will demonstrate a random distribution of arrivals and persons served, whose ratio finds direct expression in waiting time. Given a queue discipline and a certain level of arrival and service, then, waiting time will be governed by a random process. This fact sets an upper limit to predictability: the percentage of explainable waiting time variance is less than unity.

7. For facilities averaging 10, 30, 50, 70, and 95 daily arrivals, staff-patient ratios are 2.06, 3.29, 4.40, 4.84, and 5.93 respectively.

8. Mean treatment time (in minutes) corresponding to emergency room volumes of -25, 25-50, 51-100, and 101+ are 36.4, 36.5, 47.9, and 52.0 (see Gibson, Anderson, and Bugbee 1970: 206). While these figures do indicate a general trend, they must be treated with caution, for the treatment time measure includes unknown quantities of recovery time.

9. The staffing Beta for the total sample is -.137, or about one half the magnitude of the department volume effect (.264). Moreover, a separate analysis shows that staff-patient ratios predict mean department waiting time somewhat less accurately than department volume alone. (Emergency department staffing is defined as the mean number of physicians, residents, interns, registered nurses, licensed practical nurses, aides and orderlies present during the day.)

10. For facilities averaging 10, 30, 50, and 70 daily arrivals, race Betas are .120, .098, -.066, and .085, respectively. The comparable urgency Betas are .134, .054, .077, and .118.

11. Aside from the independent effects of department volume, urgency, and race, four interaction effects have been identified: (1) medical urgency and volume, (2) race and volume, (3) urgency and race, and (4) volume, urgency, and race. A separate analysis shows that the latter category accounts for about one third of the explained waiting time variance.

This datum bears implications for the way mathematical models of queuing have been used. In the formulation of these models a queue discipline of some kind is necessarily assumed; in their application, however, the assumption is not questioned, which often leads to erroneous predictions when the reality does not correspond to it. (See, for example, Lee 1966.) Some investigators have shown themselves sensitive to this danger by inquiring into servers' own perception of priority criteria (Haussmann 1970); however, this sometimes successful procedure is vulnerable to the potential discrepancy between attitude and behavior. In short, queue discipline is always an empirical problem—and often a very complex one at that; it is therefore not to be assumed without risk.

12. Because of the distribution of cases for whom medical urgency data are not available, the weighted percentage black in high-volume and low-volume facilities (table 16) does not correspond to the true sample proportions, which are 37 and 38 percent, respectively. The corresponding weighted percentages in table 16 are 32 and 39 percent. Clearly, the former figure is too low; the latter a bit too high.

That there is an equal percentage of black patients in smaller and larger emergency rooms is a surprising result. This is perhaps because so much of our thinking and research is based on the experiences of the larger urban facilities with a predominantly black clientele. We tend to forget that there are also many small and medium sized units serving a comparable client population. Similarly, many of the larger facilities accommodate patients who are mostly white.

13. The relationship between emergency department size and the medical status of its clientele has also been subject to exaggeration. In our data, 38 and 42 percent of patients in the smallest and largest facilities have been classified as nonurgent.

Chapter 6

1. This relationship cannot be attributed to differences in the size of appointment units. Of the twelve units which involved two or more clients, six had appointments at the top half of the executive hierarchy; six at the bottom half.

As a point of additional information, median client waiting times (in minutes) by separate executive rank are as follows: chairman of the board (n = 12): 14.5; vice-chairman of the board (n = 4): 6.2; president (n = 6): 8.8; senior vice-president (n = 6): 7.5; vice-president (n = 17): 5.0; assistant vice-president (n = 7): 2.5. The total median is 5.0.

2. To do the computations is a matter of comparing the frequencies of the first row *of both waiting time intervals*, then repeating the procedure for the second row.

3. Absence of information on appointment time prevents us from knowing the extent to which differential arrival times (i.e., earliness or lateness) of high and low status clients would affect the pattern observed in table 17.

4. Though the bestowal of a gift benefit may be a sign of voluntary submission and at the same time a way of elevating a recipient (Spencer 1886: 81–104), gifts may also be offered with a view to regulating the giver's indebtedness to another, and so reduce the dependency and inferiority that inheres in owing something to him. (For recent statements on this widely discussed theme, see Blau 1964b: 106–12; Schwartz 1967.)

5. This outcome is in accord with the general tendency for people to coordinate the monetary value of their gifts with the social value of recipients in order to dramatize differential (or equal) recognition and appreciation (see Schwartz 1967: 6).

6. Reference to the notion of allotment is not to suggest a finite supply in terms of which scarcity is measured and assessed; on the contrary, deference is infinite because it can be produced (i.e., expressed) whenever there is an impulse to do so (Abrahamsson 1970: 282); as such, the notion of supply makes no sense in this context at all. Rather, deferential scarcity is created by patterned willingness to express that which may be inhibited at will, and a corresponding willingness to inhibit what may at any time be given expression.

7. The general issue of reliability may now be raised. When a number of relationships fail separately to exhibit an acceptable level of significance but at the same time give rise to a coherent pattern, we can assume that a nonrandom process is operating. We deny this process only at the risk of making a Type II error (i.e., assuming that an association does not exist when it really does). After introducing a "test variable" to already significant associations, for example, the separate or partial relationships may turn out to be insignificant in statistical terms, even though they repeatedly display the same direction and magnitude as the original association. We can surely assume that insignificance is then due solely to attenuation of observations.

We enumerate below the chi-square values and significance levels for the total associations in tables 17–20. In doing so, we set no critical level: it is not a matter of "accepting" isolated relationships which attain a certain level of significance and "rejecting" those which do not. Hypotheses are evaluated in terms of the consistency with which they are supported. The following information is therefore but one source of data that bears on the stability of the results.

Chi-square values for total associations (52 observations) involving one degree of freedom are as follows: table 17: 6.52, $P = < .02$; table 18: 4.02, $P = < .05$; table 19: 7.54, $P = < .01$; table 20: 3.46, $P = < .10$. All of the above values are corrected downward for continuity.

8. This prerequisite naturally embodies one counter-image for Weber's conception of the bureaucracy (1958b: 198; 215–16):

The reduction of modern office management to rules is deeply imbedded in its very nature. . . . This stands in extreme contrast to the regulation of all relationships through individual privileges and bestowals of favor.

"Without regard for persons" is also the watchword of the "market" and, in general, of all pursuits of naked economic interests. A consistent execution of bureaucratic domination means the leveling of status "honor."

When fully developed, bureaucracy . . . stands, in a specific sense, under the principle of sine ac studio. Its specific nature, which is welcomed by capitalism, develops the more perfectly the more the bureaucracy is "dehumanized."

9. While the secretarial-receptionist staff of the organization is all female, there is not one woman among the executives or in the professional staff. This division is maintained on an imperative rather than a de facto basis. For example, one secretary who made known her intention to soon leave the organization in order to attend business school, with a hope that she might eventually return to a more responsible position within it, was promptly fired.

Each executive here refers to his secretary as his "girl," whose status and function are as undignified as such designation implies. Hired principally on the basis of physical attractiveness, female employees are trained not only to manage routine business needs but also to cater to the creature-comforts of the employer and his clients. The "girls" perform this function by gracefully dispensing food, drink, and information. They also minister more or less unwittingly, through their very appearance, which, according to executive plan, is meant to be a manifest delight to clients, if only a veiled joy to their superiors.

Thus, when the service system is mobilized to receive and accord deferential attention to a client, it is the firm's females who go into action. Client processing is in this respect a highly sexualized operation. And perhaps this is what makes so meaningful an executive's decision to offer himself as a personal escort. Involving him as it does in a purely expressive enterprise, the escort gesture *functionally* reduces him to a subservient female and, in a symbolic way, correspondingly elevates the client.

10. One limit to which these results might be generalized is the amount of congestion in the waiting room itself. As we have already pointed out, the present service system is unusual in that it plays host to so few clients. Because of its low arrival rate, the probability of clients of two or more executives being in the waiting room at any one time is quite negligible. This is a necessary condition for "audience segregation," which in this setting ensures that lesser clients rarely know how more important ones are treated and so cannot feel resentment at not being dealt with similarly. The statistical associations that we have observed might therefore be attenuated if at a typical moment the waiting area were full of differently ranked clients, for then *conspicuously* differential treatment would only cause embarrassment for those deferentially accommodated and resentment among those ignored.

Chapter 7

1. That advances in chronometry preceded the development of industrial life in metropolitan centers is a view to which Mumford (1963: 14) and de Grazia (1962: 305) commit themselves and for which Lloyd provides graphic confirmation. Lloyd (1966) shows that before the fourteenth century and the invention of the "escapement" little progress was made in time measurement precision (in terms of errors in seconds per day). Beginning with the appearance of the first pendulum clock in the seventeenth century, however, improvement up to the present has advanced at an increasing rate. This curve corresponds to the rise of urbanism and industrialism in Western societies. The relationship may be underscored by noting the diffusion of clocks and watches in the late nineteenth century, a period which Rostow (1960) shows to have preceded the economic maturation of several Western nations. It is no coincidence, then, that enemies of the industrial order look upon the timepiece as its symbol. In Jerry Rubin's utopian "Yippieland," for example, "All watches and clocks will be destroyed" (1970: 256).

2. This account, given in a lecture by David McClelland, was communicated to me by Richard Taub.

3. This result is most intriguing, insofar as it bears on the effect of waiting time. We have assumed that impatience presupposes a normative standard with respect to punctuality, and that violation of this standard gives rise to the most intense dissatisfaction with delay. If this were so—if impatience were relative to the discrepancy between appointment time and the actual moment at which service is offered—then we would expect to find (1) the strongest association between waiting time and dissatisfaction among patients with prearranged appointments and (2) the strongest association between appointment status and dissatisfaction among patients who have been delayed the longest. In fact, however, there is no consistent relationship between appointment status and impatience, and none between waiting time and impatience by appointment status (table 21). This is to say that the effect of waiting time is independent of a normative or appointment anchor point. What seems to matter is delay itself, along with its religious or cultural meaning, regardless of expectations arising from a scheduled appointment. This finding would not be inconsistent with the possible fact that patients may *account* for their displeasure by invoking the normative appointment standard; it does suggest, however, that such an interpretation is no more than an account, and that what really hurts is waiting itself.

In this regard, another expectation was discredited. We initially assumed that each increment in cost brings with it less dissatisfaction (the principle of diminishing marginal disutility of increasing amounts of harm), which means that as waiting time is extended, impatience would tend to increase at a decreasing rate. However, the data show this relationship to be distinctly linear under all circumstances.

4. The cut-off points for poverty level by family sizes 1 to 7+ are $2,600, $3,700, $4,500, $5,700, $6,600, $7,500, and $9,100.

5. The direction of this relationship may have something to do with the black's recently heightened awareness of his entitlements to economic and social rewards. In an era of black liberation it is no surprise that waiting, which is a direct expression of dependence and subjugation, is found to be so oppressive.

6. Of these three variables, age alone is independently associated with impatience. Those under 65 consistently express the most distress—twice as much, on the average—as persons over 65. The greater tolerance of delay is found in the group most likely to be retired and free of obligations to dependents; that is to say, those for whom time is most plentiful. The most patient, then, are the people who give up the least by being delayed.

Chapter 8

1. To this corresponds immobilization in the purely geographical sense. Though he was initially mobile, the waiting role which the client eventually assumes may render him quite stationary, for if he leaves the waiting channel he may lose his turn and forfeit both the service he desires and the investment (in time) made before his departure. Similarly, those who conduct business over the phone may be asked to wait while the other party takes a temporary leave of his end of the line in order to look into the matter in question; it is

discovered at this point that mobility is limited by the length of the phone cord. Freedom is gained only when the server returns to the phone to complete the transaction. This problem is only partly obviated by the introduction of the telephone extension cord. In addition, secretaries or operators may be instructed in techniques for holding a client in this uncomfortable position. The practice of periodically advising him of the status of his call with the reassuring "The line's still busy; I'll keep trying," and "Still ringing," is a standard one.

2. Distinguishing between dominant and subordinate involvements, Goffman (1963: 44) writes:

A dominating involvement is one whose claims upon an individual the social occasion obliges him to be ready to recognize; a subordinate involvement is one he is allowed to sustain only to the degree, and during the time, that his attention is patently not required by the involvement that dominates him. Subordinate involvements are sustained in a muted, modulated, and intermittent fashion, expressing in their style a continuous regard and deference for the official, dominating activity at hand. Thus, while waiting to see an official, an individual may converse with a friend, read a magazine or doodle with a pencil, sustaining these engrossing claims on attention only until his turn is called, when he is obliged to put aside his timepassing activity even though it is unfinished.

3. In banks, "the shorter the line the larger the body space allowed and the less distinct the line formation remained. As lines became longer the body space maintained between customers ... is shortened" (Prather 1972: 8).

4. For a general discussion of intrinsic and extrinsic *rewards*, see Blau (1964b: 35–38).

5. This principle is well illustrated in the skillfully operated restaurant which, on busy days, succeeds in holding those who because of slow service are inclined to get up and leave. The trick is to promptly place at the customer's table items such as plates, silverware, and water so as to dramatize his membership on the service list, to which he consequently feels bound despite a disposition to leave when he finally realizes that he will have to wait a very long time before he gets anything else (personal communication from Gideon Aran). This sort of deliberation may be inferred from queuing patterns in many other contexts. For a second instance, at an airline check-in counter, Lee (1966: 130) reports that "once a passenger had joined a queue, he appeared very often unwilling to leave it for another. There were numerous instances of a queue at counter 7, for example, and no queues at counters 4 and 3. [Yet] the passengers remained where they were."

6. A general point, first enunciated by Simmel (1950a: 380), embraces this observation: "The rise of a relationship, to be sure, requires certain positive and negative conditions, and the absence of even one of them may, at once, preclude its development. Yet once started, it is by no means always destroyed by the subsequent disappearance of that condition which, earlier, it could not have overcome."

References

Abrahamsson, Bengt. 1970. "Homans on Exchange: Hedonism Revived." *American Journal of Sociology* 76 (September): 273–85.

Adler, Alfred. 1916. *The Neurotic Constitution.* New York: Moffat, Yard.

Alexander, C. Norman, and Simpson, Richard. 1964. "Balance Theory and Distributive Justice." *Sociological Inquiry* 34 (Spring): 182–92.

Alihan, Milla. 1970. *Corporate Etiquette.* New York: Weybright and Talley.

Andersen, R.; Kravitz, J.; and Anderson, O. W. 1971. "The Public's View of the Crisis in Medical Care: An Impetus for Changing Delivery Systems?" *Economic and Business Bulletin* 24 (Fall): 44–52.

Arthur, R., and Caputo, R. 1959. *Interrogation for Investigators.* New York: Copp.

Becker, Gary. 1965. "A Theory of the Allocation of Time." *Economic Journal* (September): 493–517.

Beckett, Samuel. 1954. *Waiting for Godot.* New York: Grove.

Bell, Daniel. 1973. *The Coming of Post-Industrial Society.* New York: Basic Books, Inc.

Bettelheim, Bruno. 1960. *The Informed Heart.* Glencoe, Ill.: The Free Press.

————. 1965. *Love Is Not Enough.* New York: Collier Books.

Blau, Peter. 1964a. "Justice in Social Exchange." *Sociological Inquiry* 34 (Spring): 193–206.

————. 1964b. *Exchange and Power in Social Life.* New York: John Wiley and Sons.

————. 1970. "A Formal Theory of Differentiation in Organizations." *American Sociological Review* 35 (April): 201–18.

Bradford, Jean. 1971. "Getting the Most out of Odd Moments." *Reader's Digest* (June): 82–84.

Brown, Roger. 1965. *Social Psychology*. New York: The Free Press.

Cartter, Alan M. 1966. *An Assessment of Quality in Graduate Education*. Washington, D.C.: American Council on Education.

Cooley, Charles Horton. 1964. *Human Nature and the Social Order*. New York: Schocken Books.

de Grazia, Sebastian. 1962. *Of Time, Work and Leisure*. New York: The Twentieth Century Fund.

Doyle, Bertram. 1937. *The Etiquette of Race Relations in the South*. Chicago: University of Chicago Press.

Fenichel, Otto. 1945. *The Psychoanalytic Theory of Neurosis*. New York: W. W. Norton, Inc.

Fenwick, Millicent. 1968. *Vogue's Book of Etiquette*. New York: Simon and Schuster.

Festinger, Leon. 1957. *A Theory of Cognitive Dissonance*. Evanston, Ill.: Row, Peterson.

Foy, Eddie. 1957. "The Iroquois Theater Fire." In *Collective Behavior*, edited by Ralph H. Turner and Lewis M. Killian, pp. 96–97. Englewood Cliffs: Prentice-Hall, Inc.

Freud, Sigmund. 1963. "From the History of an Infantile Neurosis." In *Three Case Histories*, edited by Philip Rieff, pp. 187–316. New York: Collier Books.

Fromm, Erich. 1941. *Escape from Freedom*. New York: Avon Library.

Gibson, Geoffrey; Anderson, Odin; and Bugbee, George. 1970. *Emergency Medical Services in the Chicago Area*. Center for Health Administration Studies, University of Chicago.

Glaser, Barney, and Strauss, Anselm. 1965. *Awareness of Dying*. Chicago: Aldine.

Glaser, Barney. 1972. *The Patsy and the Subcontractor*. Mill Valley, Calif.: Sociology Press.

Goffman, Erving. 1956. "The Nature of Deference and Demeanor." *American Anthropologist* 58 (June): 473–502.

————. 1959. *The Presentation of Self in Everyday Life*. Garden City, N.Y.: Doubleday and Company, Inc.

————. 1963. *Behavior in Public Places*. New York: The Free Press.

————. 1971. *Relations in Public*. New York: Basic Books, Inc.

Hall, Edward T. 1959. *The Silent Language*. Greenwich: Fawcett Publications, Inc.

————. 1966. *The Hidden Dimension.* Garden City: Doubleday and Company, Inc.

Haussmann, R. K. Dieter. 1970. "Waiting Time as an Index of Quality of Nursing Care." *Health Services Research* (Summer): 92–105.

Homans, George C. 1961. *Social Behavior: Its Elementary Forms.* New York: Harcourt, Brace and World.

Lee, Alec M. 1966. *Applied Queuing Theory.* London: Macmillan.

Levine, Irving R. 1959. *Main Street, U.S.S.R.* Garden City: Doubleday and Company, Inc.

————. 1963. *Main Street Italy.* Garden City: Doubleday and Company, Inc.

Liberman, E. G. 1968–69. "The Queue: Anamnesis, Diagnosis, Therapy." *Soviet Review* 9 (Winter): 12–16.

Linder, Staffan B. 1970. *The Harried Leisure Class.* New York: Columbia University Press.

Lloyd, H. Alan. 1966. "Timekeepers—A Historical Sketch." In *The Voices of Time,* edited by J. T. Fraser, pp. 388–400. New York: George Braziller.

Lohman, Joseph D. 1957. "The Role of the Police Officer in Crowd Control." In *Collective Behavior,* edited by Ralph H. Turner and Lewis M. Killian, pp. 144–47. Englewood Cliffs: Prentice-Hall, Inc.

Malinowski, Bronislaw. 1958. *Magic, Science and Religion.* Glencoe, Ill.: The Free Press.

Mann, Leon. 1969. "Queue Culture: The Waiting Line as a Social System." *American Journal of Sociology* 75 (November): 340–54.

Mann, Leon, and Taylor, K. R. 1969. "Queue Counting: The Effect of Motives upon Estimates of Numbers in Waiting Lines." *Journal of Personality and Social Psychology* 12 (June): 95–103.

Mead, Margaret. 1955. *Cultural Patterns and Technical Change.* New York: The New American Library.

Meerloo, Joost. 1966. "The Time Sense in Psychiatry." In *The Voices of Time,* edited by J. T. Fraser, pp. 235–52. New York: George Braziller.

Merton, Robert K. 1957. "Priorities in Scientific Discovery: A Chapter in the Sociology of Science." *American Sociological Review* 22 (December): 635–59. Also published as chapter 14 in Robert K. Merton, *The*

Sociology of Science. Chicago: University of Chicago Press, 1973.

Mintz, Alexander. 1951. "Non-adaptive Group Behavior." *Journal of Abnormal and Social Psychology* 46 (April): 150–59.

Moore, Wilbert E. 1963. *Man, Time and Society.* New York: Wiley.

Mumford, Lewis. 1963. *Technics and Civilization.* New York: Harcourt, Brace and World, Inc.

Parkinson, C. Northcote. 1962. *Parkinson's Law.* Boston: Houghton Mifflin.

Parsons Talcott. 1951a. *The Social System.* New York: The Free Press.

Parsons, Talcott. 1951b. "Values, Motives and Systems of Action." In *Toward a General Theory of Action,* edited by Talcott Parsons and Edward A. Shils, pp. 49–278. New York: Harper and Row.

Parsons, Talcott, and Smelser, Neil. 1957. *Economy and Society.* New York: The Free Press.

Perlman, Mark. 1969. "Rationing of Medical Resources: The Complexities of the Supply and Demand Problem." *The Sociological Review.* Monograph 14 (September): 105–19.

Post, Emily. 1965. *Emily Post's Etiquette: The Blue Book of Social Usage.* New York: Funk and Wagnalls Company, Inc.

Prather, Jane. 1972. "Sociological Observations of Privacy Behavior in a Bank Lobby." Paper presented at the Annual Meeting of the American Sociological Association, August 28–31.

Raymond, Louise. 1965. *Good Housekeeping's Book of Today's Etiquette.* New York: Harper & Row.

Reif, F. 1961. "The Competitive World of the Pure Scientist." *Science* 134 (December): 1957–62.

Rodman, Hyman. 1970. "The Moral Responsibility of Journal Editors and Referees." *The American Sociologist* 5 (November): 351–57.

Rokeach, Milton. 1960. *The Open and Closed Mind.* New York: Basic Books, Inc.

Rostow, W. W. 1960. *The Stages of Economic Growth.* Cambridge: Cambridge University Press.

Roth, Julius. 1971. "Utilization of the Hospital Emergency

Department." *Journal of Health and Social Behavior* 12 (December): 312–20.

———. 1972. "Some Contingencies of the Moral Evaluation and Control of Clientele: The Case of the Hospital Emergency Service." *American Journal of Sociology* 77 (November): 839–56.

Rubin, Jerry. 1970. *Do It!* New York: Ballantine Books.

Saaty, Thomas L. 1961. *Elements of Queuing Theory.* New York: McGraw-Hill Co., Inc.

Schwartz, Barry. 1967. "The Social Psychology of the Gift." *American Journal of Sociology* 73 (July): 1–11.

———. 1970. "Notes on the Sociology of Sleep." *Sociological Quarterly* (Fall): 485–99.

Shils, Edward. 1970. "Deference." In *The Logic of Social Hierarchies,* edited by Edward O. Laumann et al., pp. 420–48. Chicago: Markham Publishing Company.

Simmel, Georg. 1950a. "Faithfulness and Gratitude." In *The Sociology of Georg Simmel,* edited by Kurt H. Wolff, pp. 379–95. New York: The Free Press.

———. 1950b. "The Metropolis and Mental Life." In *The Sociology of Georg Simmel,* edited by Kurt H. Wolff, pp. 409–24. New York: The Free Press.

———. (1907) 1970. "Exchange." Unabridged translation by Donald N. Levine.

———. 1971. "Exchange." In *George Simmel: On Individuality and Social Forms,* edited by Donald N. Levine. Chicago: University of Chicago Press.

Singer, Jerome. 1961. "Imagination and Waiting Ability in Young Children." *Journal of Personality* 29 (March-December): 396–413.

Skinner, B. F. 1953. *Science and Human Behavior.* New York: The Macmillan Company.

Slater, Philip. 1963. "On Social Regression." *American Sociological Review* 28 (June): 339–64.

Smelser, Neil J. 1962. *Theory of Collective Behavior.* New York: The Free Press.

Solzhenitsyn, Aleksandr. 1968a. *The Cancer Ward.* New York: Dial.

———. 1968b. *The First Circle.* New York: Harper & Row.

Spencer, Herbert. 1886. *The Principles of Sociology.* Volume 2. New York: D. Appleton and Company.

Stinchcombe, Arthur. 1970. "Organized Dependency Relations

and Social Stratification." In *The Logic of Social Hierarchies,* edited by Edward Laumann et al., pp. 95–99. Chicago: Markham.

Sudnow, David. 1967. *Passing On.* Englewood Cliffs: Prentice-Hall, Inc.

Tawney, R. H. 1931. *Equality.* London: Allen & Unwin.

Thompson, James D. 1967. *Organizations in Action.* New York: McGraw-Hill Company.

Turner, Ralph, and Killian, Lewis. 1957. *Collective Behavior.* Englewood Cliffs: Prentice-Hall, Inc.

Weber, Max. 1958a. *The Protestant Ethic and the Spirit of Capitalism.* New York: Charles Scribner's Sons.

————. 1958b. "Bureaucracy." In *From Max Weber,* edited by Hans Gerth and C. Wright Mills, pp. 196–244. New York: Oxford University Press.

————. 1964. *The Theory of Social and Economic Organization.* Glencoe, Ill.: The Free Press.

Zamiatin, Eugene. 1924. *We.* New York: E. P. Dutton and Co., Inc.

Index

213